God's Solutions for Your Life

God *Has a* Plan *for* Your Life

&

How to Let God Solve Your Problems

Charles F. Stanley

Thomas Nelson
Since 1798

NASHVILLE   DALLAS   MEXICO CITY   RIO DE JANEIRO

God Has a Plan for Your Life and *How to Let God Solve Your Problems* © 2008 by Great Commission Media

All rights reserved. No portion of this book may be reproduced, stored in a retrieval system, or transmitted in any form or by any means—electronic, mechanical, photocopy, recording, scanning, or other—except for brief quotations in critical reviews or articles, without the prior written permission of the publisher.

Published in Nashville, Tennessee, by Thomas Nelson. Thomas Nelson is a registered trademark of Thomas Nelson, Inc.

Thomas Nelson, Inc., titles may be purchased in bulk for educational, business, fund-raising, or sales promotional use. For information, please e-mail SpecialMarkets@ThomasNelson.com.

Unless otherwise noted, Scripture quotations are taken from the NEW AMERICAN STANDARD BIBLE®. © The Lockman Foundation 1960, 1962, 1963, 1968, 1971, 1972, 1973, 1975, 1977. Used by permission.

Scripture quotations marked NIV are from the HOLY BIBLE: NEW INTERNATIONAL VERSION®. © 1973, 1978, 1984 by International Bible Society. Used by permission of Zondervan Publishing House. All rights reserved.

Scripture quotations marked NKJV are from the NEW KING JAMES VERSION. © 1982 by Thomas Nelson, Inc. Used by permission. All rights reserved.

ISBN: 978-0-8499-2152-0 (*God's Solutions for Your Life* SE)

Printed in the United States of America

11 12 BTY 7 6 5 4 3 2

GOD *Has a* PLAN *for* YOUR LIFE

The Discovery That Makes
All the Difference

"I know the plans that I have for you," declares the LORD.
Jeremiah 29:11

Contents

Does God Have a Plan for Me?

Does God have a purpose and a plan for my life? If so, can I know it?" Each time I hear these two questions, I answer the same way: yes, He does. In fact, His personal promise to you is that He does have a purpose and a plan for your life (Jer. 29:11). While you may not know or understand all the twists and turns of life, you can be sure of one thing: the same God who breathed life into you loves you enough to plan for your future. He has promised that if you will seek Him, you will find Him, and you also will discover His will for your life.

Many people spend a lot of time thinking about how God's will is a mystery that cannot be unlocked. This simply is not true. We can know the plans He has for us. We may not know all the details because God keeps some aspects of His will to Himself, but we can know the right path to take in every situation.

Years ago, I wrote a small book entitled *Discovering God's Will.* In it, I included some of the questions people asked on a regular basis. Each one involved some aspect of God's will for their lives. At that time, most of the questions focused on potential marriage partners, raising children, and selecting the right vocation.

"I was offered a new job in another state. There are a lot of pluses about it. Can God help me make a wise decision?"

"My daughter is a high school senior and has the opportunity to attend several colleges this fall. How can I know which one is right for her?"

"Should I marry this girl? I really think God has brought us together, but I would like to know God's mind on our future together."

Today, however, many questions we face have changed. Following the world events of the past few years, the questions are much more intense and include ones such as the following:

"Yesterday, I received word that I was going to be laid off from my job. My wife is out of work also, and I don't know how we will pay our mortgage. Does God have a plan for us? I need to know because I feel so hopeless."

"I'm thirty-one years old, and my doctor told me last week that I have cancer. I don't understand. I love God and have been living my life for Him. Why is He allowing this to happen? Does He have a purpose for my suffering?"

"Last week, my doorbell rang and I opened the door to a sight that I feared would come. Two army officers stood before me with the news that my son had been killed in battle. My grief is so great. I don't understand God's will at all. My son was so young. What is God doing? Is there a way that He will use this for some purpose in the future?"

"I never realized I could feel so lonely. However, after my husband left me last year, I have struggled with deep feelings of loneliness and even fear. Some of my Christian friends have tried to help, but many of them are busy with their own families. Does God still have a plan for me? Will I ever feel happy and alive again?"

"For several years, I used various drugs. Today, thanks to God's help and the support of my church family, I am drug-free. However, now I feel so shameful. Can God still use me? Does He have a plan for my life? Is there hope for my future?"

Without a doubt, today, more and more people are wondering if God is aware of their situation and the problems they are facing. However, the deeper question is, "Does He love me and have a purpose for my life?"

Let me start this book with some very good news. In spite of any difficulty or sin that you may have faced, God still has a fantastic plan in mind for your life. This is His personal promise for you. It is His plan to give you hope and a future, and it is His goal to lead you through the difficult times as well as the good times so that you will fulfill His purpose in this life. In Proverbs, He says that when we turn to Him and place the focus of our hearts on Him, "He will make your paths straight" (3:5–6).

For someone reading these words, the idea of traveling a straight path is very encouraging, especially if you spent years wandering in circles that had you on pathways God never designed for you to travel. However, all of that is about to change as you discover His will for your life, which includes a plan that is tailored perfectly to suit you. Many people want to know, "How can I be sure that I am doing the right thing? Will God tell me?" The answer is yes!

He will never leave you groping for answers. You may have to spend some time seeking His face for answers to your prayers, but when you do, you will never be disappointed. He is the only One who knows the plans that He has for us and how they can be fulfilled. They are plans that contain renewed peace and joy.

It is my heart's prayer that everyone who reads this book will allow God to demonstrate His infinite love and care in a fresh new way. Without a doubt, once you accept Christ as your Savior, the most important aspect of the Christian life is learning that He has a will and purpose not only for your eternal life, but also for every situation you face each day.

It all begins with faith in an all-powerful, loving Savior who has your very best in mind—always. Once you place your faith in Him, nothing can hold you back from gaining the peace and contentment that He has for you. My question to you is this: are you ready to take the first step to discovering exactly what God has planned for you? Don't miss another moment that could be spent in the blessing He promises each one of us.

Charles F. Stanley

CHAPTER ONE
The Big Picture

Does God have a plan for me?" the young man asked. His face was etched with worry and regret. He had come to know Christ as his Savior years before during a youth rally, but now, sitting in my office, he was not only on the verge of doubting his salvation but also God's love for him. He could not see past the sin that was in his life, nor could he accept God's forgiveness, and this was choking the spiritual life out of him.

I reassured him that while there were consequences to sin, God still had a plan and a purpose for his life. He never gives up on us. Even though he had made mistakes, and at one point ignored God's leading, the Lord loved him and heard his prayers. God would not ignore him or push him aside.

A *Future and a Hope*

"God loves you," I reassured him (Jer. 31:3; John 3:16). "He created you, and He is not about to give up on you—not now—not ever. You can depend on this." Instantly, silence filled the room. I could sense that God had broken through, and for the first time in a very long time, this young man's mind and heart were tuned in to the voice of God. Then I repeated a familiar verse to him—one that most of us have come to know by heart, Jeremiah 29:11: "'I know the plans that I have for you,' declares the LORD, 'plans for welfare and not for calamity to give you a future and a hope.'"

Leaning forward, I looked straight into my young friend's eyes and said, "You realize this is not Charles Stanley talking. This is God speaking to you. I don't have all the answers, but there is one thing that I do know and that is this: God knows exactly where you are at this very minute, and He understands your every struggle (Ps. 46:1). He is the one who has all the answers you need, and each one is found within His Word. He may not like where your life is right now, but He is not going to abandon you (John 14:18). If you will trust Him, He will begin to work in your life. Then you will see His plan and will for your life unfold in a mighty way. This is His promise to each one of us."

My words were hitting their right mark because the young man relaxed and drew in a deep breath. "You mean there is hope for my life?"

"Absolutely," I said without hesitation. "With God, there always is hope, and He has a plan in mind for our tomorrows."

There were another few minutes of silence; finally, he looked up at me and asked, "Okay, where do I begin?" Then I knew he was ready to start an amazing journey with the Lord—one that, if he held to the right course, would allow him to experience God's love and provision in a way unlike anything he had ever known. That afternoon, as I closed the door to my study, I wondered how many other people were facing exactly what this young man was facing—a sense of hopelessness and a longing to know God's promise and purpose for their lives.

The Discovery

Discovering God's will hinges on two things: a desire to live your life for Christ and not for yourself, and your ability to understand the nature of His will and purpose. These two aspects affect every area of life. First of all, we need to understand the fact that God is committed to our success—not in a financial sense, though He is not opposed to a person making money. He is the one who gives us the ability to make wealth (Deut. 8:18). His objection comes when the desires of our hearts are set on something other than Him. This could include a material possession or an employment position. It also includes people, hobbies, and goals or dreams that simply are not God's best for us. In fact, anything that takes His place in our lives as number one is subject to His scrutiny.

The apostle Peter would have understood perfectly what my young friend was facing. When he first met Jesus alongside the Sea of Galilee, he was nothing more than a fisherman who had a net full of dreams and very few fish. Within Peter's life, Jesus saw amazing potential, and as He stepped up on the bow of Peter's boat, He surely noticed the rough intensity that filled His future disciple's eyes. Can you imagine Jesus smiling? I can, because He knew the plans He had in mind for Peter, just as He knows the plans He has for each one of us.

We should never allow the enemy to stop us at the doorway of opportunity by tempting us to struggle with feelings of doubt and low self-esteem. Instead, we act wisely when we obey God's command just as Peter did when Christ instructed him to sail out into deep waters (Luke 5:4). Think about it for a moment. Peter was an expert fisherman. Yet he had been out on the Sea of Galilee all night and had not caught a single fish. How could he possibly know God was setting the stage for his call into a ministry that would impact the world with such force that it would never be the same again?

Each one of us can probably remember a time when we have argued with God. We could sense the Lord leading us to do a certain thing, call a certain person, or trust Him in a certain situation, but we did not know if what we were hearing or feeling was the right thing to do. Peter was no exception. He was ready to debate Jesus' request and to begin to list the reasons why it was senseless to return to the same place he was the night before. However, at the same time, Christ's request touched something deep inside of him, and suddenly, he had a desire to obey Jesus simply because he knew the One who was doing the talking. The Lord instructed Peter to "put out into deep water, and let down the nets for a catch" (Luke 5:4). Christ's words to Peter were really not a request. Requests offer options, but Jesus did not offer another plan.

Fishermen with any experience, especially on the Sea of Galilee, knew that fish were caught in shallow water and not in cool and unpredictable deep water. However, Peter obeyed the Lord's command, and it was the best decision he ever made. You will never go wrong obeying God. You may not know exactly where you are going, but you can be sure of one thing: when you get to the place He has called you to go, you will experience a miraculous blessing.

The Right Choice

We can imagine that for a few tense moments, Peter's eyes locked on the Savior's eyes. The sun was beating down, and Peter was exhausted. He had listened to Jesus teach to those who were gathered around the shoreline. Deep inside, perhaps, all he wanted was to go home and fall into his bed and sleep for a few hours before returning to his boat and work. Drawing in a deep breath of the sea's air, he nodded slowly and then agreed to Jesus' command.

Peter's response was perfect and right on track for an extreme blessing. "Master, we worked hard all night and caught nothing, but I will do as you say and let down the nets" (Luke 5:5). If you are looking for the key to Peter's success, here it is: "But I will do as you say and let down the nets." Obedience always is the first step to discovering God's plan for your life.

Jesus did not step up to Peter's boat and say, "If you will allow Me to climb on board and speak to the crowd, we'll go for a boat ride that will change your entire destiny." Instead, He asked Peter if He could use his boat. He needed a platform not only for the miracle that was about to take place, but He also wanted to speak to the people who had gathered. Wherever Jesus went, a crowd of people followed. These were men and women who were hungry for truth and for a Savior. Peter was among this same group. He longed for Messiah to come just as others did, but at that very moment, he had no idea that the answer to his prayers was now standing in his small fishing boat.

Once his fishing boat was away from the shore, he lifted the sails of the small vessel and headed out for deeper water. He was living in obedience to God's will and did not even have a clue that this was what he was doing. His simple act of obedience was positioning him for a great blessing.

As he dropped the net over the side of the boat, he probably glanced back to the distant shoreline and wondered what his friends were thinking. One thing that can block us from fulfilling God's promise for our lives is becoming entangled in what others think about what we are doing. If God has positioned us in a certain place, we must leave all the details to Him. With total abandonment, Peter obeyed Christ. Imagine the emotion that went through him a few minutes later when his nets began to fill up with fish. In fact, the catch was so large he immediately shouted back to his friends—James and John, whom Jesus later called the "sons of thunder"—to come and help him. Then he fell at the Lord's feet and said, "Go away from me Lord, for I am a sinful man!" (Luke 5:8).

Blessings for Obedience

Here is the beauty of God's intimate love for you, especially if you have ever been concerned about how He views your life. Jesus responded to Peter in a way that turned his life upside down, "Do not fear, from now on you will be catching men" (Luke 5:10). The New International Version of the Bible says, "You will catch men." In other words, you will catch men for My heavenly Father's glory and no longer be caught up emotionally and mentally with the things of this world.

At the close of the scene, we are left with a memorable image: "When they had brought their boats to land, they left everything and followed Him" (v. 11). It was not the end of the story. Instead, it was just the beginning of God's will being revealed to Peter and those who chose to follow the Savior.

We live in a society that wants instant results—instant food, instant access to computer programs, instant service. If it can't happen quickly, we will usually be tempted to become frustrated and walk away. If we see something we want, we can find a way to purchase it. However, experiencing the fullness of God's will is not something that happens immediately. It takes time—a lifetime. He may give us an idea as to what His will is, but it takes a life of devotion to uncover His complete purpose and plan for our lives. Peter could only handle what Jesus revealed to him at the moment. There will be times in our lives when God will instruct us to step forward. His express will is for us to obey Him. We may not understand what He is calling us to do. However, at this point, His goal for us is obedience. Therefore, we must step forward, trusting Him for the future.

God has a plan, and it should be our goal to live out that plan to the best of our knowledge and ability. Without a doubt, there will be times when we get off course. Later, we will see how Peter did just that. However, we'll read how the Lord moved quickly to get His disciple back on track and back into the center of God's will. Many people mistakenly believe that Jesus is too busy to walk with them through difficult times. They forget that He is their ever-present Advocate before His heavenly Father's throne.

Jesus prays unceasingly for us. The author of Hebrews writes, "Therefore He is able also to save forever those who draw near to God through Him, since He always lives to make intercession for them" (7:25). When we yield to temptation, Christ is our advocate before God's throne of mercy and grace (1 John 2:1). You may feel as though you do not have a friend you can turn to for help and encouragement. However, you do. Jesus Christ promises to listen to your every prayer, and He will never leave you. Instead, He will remain even closer to you than a brother (Prov. 18:24). This is why we long to fulfill God's will. Once we draw near to His presence and experience His goodness extended toward us, we will want to be with Him every day.

We also will want to spend time with Him in prayer and studying His Word. I often tell people who truly want to know His will for their lives to study His Word, pray, and seek His wisdom for their situations. When we do, He will answer our prayers and reveal the portion of His will that we need to know.

God sees the big picture of our lives and knows all

that it will take to get us to a place where we will fulfill His will. He knows how He wants the events of our lives to end. He also knows how to position us so that we fulfill His plan and glorify Him. The purpose of our lives is not to serve ourselves by focusing on what we feel is important and holds value. From God's perspective, this is a very narrow view of the life that He has given us to live. Instead of thinking, *What about me and my desires?*, the right question to ask is, "Lord, what is Your desire for my life? Please show me Your plan, and make Your will absolutely clear so I can do it."

CHAPTER TWO
God's Promise Fulfilled

There is no doubt that God has a plan for our lives, and He wants us to discover it and live in the middle of it. At times, He may reveal to us a portion of His will. We will know that God has brought us to a certain point but not know all that is connected with being there. Remember, Abraham did not wait for God's promise to be completely revealed to him before he obeyed the Lord. Instead, he left his home believing in the One who had called him.

David was anointed king over Israel. However, it was many years before he sat on the nation's throne. These were years of extreme danger and disappointment. He was forced to run for his life from an angry king whose sole existence was wrapped up in ending David's life. Before

David could do God's will, he had to be trained by adversity, disappointment, and, at times, extreme difficulty. Was he outside the will of God? There were moments when he made decisions that were not the best, but David kept pace with God's will even when he could not see how he would make it through the next day.

Like David, you may be walking through a deep valley and wondering if you are in God's will. Remember, He has promised to guide you and lead you to a place where you will fulfill His will and purpose for your life. David writes, "Even though I walk through the valley of the shadow of death, I fear no evil; for You are with me" (Ps. 23:4). David was walking through the valley and knew that he would emerge victorious on the other side of his problems. He did not become a sorrowful person. He became a man after God's own heart and learned to do God's will regardless of his circumstances, and we can do the same (Acts 13:22).

Learn to Trust

David also was the author of a majority of the psalms, and in Psalm 40, he writes, "I delight to do Your will, O my God" (v. 8). Then in Psalm 143:10, his words form a personal prayer, "Teach me to do Your will, for You are my God; let Your good Spirit lead me on level ground." God answered David's prayers and continued to lead him through a lifetime of trials and victories. The question we need to answer is, are we willing for God to do the same thing in our lives?

He has a will for every single one of us, and the prayer of our hearts always should be, "Lord, teach me to do Your will." When we pray this way, we are praying the same way Jesus prayed before facing Calvary: "Not My will, but Yours be done" (Luke 22:42). This is a prayer of surrender—surrender to God's perfect will and not our human desires.

Even Jesus, God's Son, understood that God had a plan in mind for His life. While He did not know all the steps in that plan, He knew He could trust the One who was in control of His destiny. Do you know the same thing? Can you say without a doubt that you are fully surrendered to the Lord so that He can reveal His will in and through your life?

Years ago, after one of our mission conferences, a young woman came to me and told me that she felt as though God was calling her to become a missionary. I'm always cautious when I talk with people about what God is doing in their lives because there is no way to know for certain what He is up to until we surrender to Him and then allow Him to make His will perfectly clear. I also want to make sure that God's will is not limited to being a pastor or some ministry-related work. God leads many people to work in secular environments while serving Him through their churches and other ministries.

I listened as this woman expressed the great turmoil that was going on in her life. On one hand, she was willing to say yes to God; on the other, she was afraid of the consequences of such a decision. It would mean a total lifestyle change beginning with her returning to college. I suggested that she take time to get alone with God and pray. I told her, "He has a will for your life, and if you set a goal to be still before Him and study His Word, He will reveal it to you."

Weeks later, I found out that she had taken my advice to be alone with the Lord and seek His will in this situation. God made it clear through His Word that He was calling her to trust Him and serve Him in the area of missions. Whenever we make a decision to do what He is showing us to do, then we experience His blessings. We may not know all there is to know about His will, but we can say yes and begin an awesome journey that leads to fulfillment and peace because we know that we have obeyed God.

Take the First Step

You may be thinking, *Well, I would take the first step, if I only knew what the plan looked like*. Remember, Peter did not know. He just wanted to obey Christ's call to him. God does not show us more than what we can handle. He only revealed a portion of His will to Moses. Then, like David, he was forced to live years in a wilderness situation that probably left him wondering if he would ever do what God had called him to do. The same was true of Abraham and Joseph. Both of these men were given glimpses of God's plan for their lives, but they had to "winter" with God and wait for His appointed time. Timing is everything to God. He knows the perfect moment to call to you and the perfect moment for you to answer Him.

When we are willing to listen and wait for His will, God will begin to unfold His plan and purpose for us. We know the right steps to take because, with each move we make, we will sense Him saying, "Yes, this is what I have planned for your life."

If you have never accepted Jesus Christ as your Savior, then you do not know how to enter or enjoy the promise that God has given you (John 3:3). I can tell you without a doubt that His will for you at this moment is for you to enter into a personal relationship with Him by accepting His Son as your Savior. Once you do this, you will be ready to begin to discover His will along with His exciting purpose and plan for your future.

Before you read any further, take a moment to pray this life-changing prayer:

Dear God, I am so grateful that Your love for me is unconditional and that You have made an eternal promise to me—one that cannot be withdrawn. I realize that You also have an eternal plan in mind for my life, and it is one of hope and promise (Jer. 29:11). I bow before You and ask that You would save me from an eternal death. I give my life to You and pray for Your cleansing touch over my life and ask that You would place within my heart a deep abiding love for You and Your Word. Thank You that You sent Your Son to die for me on Calvary's cross. I accept His death as payment for my sins. I also acknowledge my need of a Savior and ask that He would come into my life through the presence of the Holy Spirit. I am grateful that You love me enough to never leave me and that You only desire what is best for my life. Please reveal Your promise to me—the gift You have given through Your Son, so that

I may live my life in the light of Your will. I pray this in Jesus' name. Amen.

God's Faithfulness Revealed

As I was thinking about the writing of this book, God reminded me of a time when He met my needs in a dramatic way. When I was fourteen years old, He called me to preach. I knew this was His will for my life. However, by the time I was seventeen and a senior in high school, I began to wonder how He would pull everything together in order for me to go to college and study to enter the ministry. At the time, the only job I had was delivering papers, and it did not produce enough income for me to save for my education.

Many of the people who read this book can identify with my situation. You know that God has placed a goal in front of you, but you don't know how it will take place. Limited resources and a limited view of the future can leave us wondering if God is really calling us in a certain direction. However, we do not have to wonder when we know in our hearts that He has confirmed His will. At a point like this, the only thing to do is to obey and step forward by faith. However, this does not mean that He wants us to exercise our faith by using credit cards and borrowing money that we cannot repay. He is very creative, and He provides for our needs in amazing ways. Often, people come to me and tell me how they know God has called them to the mission field or to preach or to work for Him in another way, but they hesitate. Fear grabs at their minds and hearts, and they become stuck in their walk with the Lord. They feel trapped by their circumstances because they haven't caught the vision that God has for their lives.

As I turned my situation over to the Lord in prayer, I knew that if He had called me to preach, He would equip me for the task. Faith plays an important role in accessing God's promises. Many times, if we doubt His faithfulness and goodness to us, we will miss the blessings that He has for us. Sadly, we also miss doing His will.

As I prepared for my high school graduation, I waited for the Lord to show me what He wanted me to do next. He led me to apply to the college that I wanted to attend. I may have had very little money, but I had a great deal of faith in God's ability. Trusting God to supply all your needs is the key to walking each day in the center of His will.

My financial shortfall was not a deficit because it did not reflect the infinite resources that are available to all who believe in Christ. At the end of each month, I had enough money to buy the clothes I needed for school and my lunches. However, there was not much left over for anything else. I knew my family could not help me, but I was not discouraged. My youthful faith was set on God, and I was sure that He would open the door that I needed to walk through at just the right moment. I was not wrong.

One night as I finished delivering papers, I stopped to talk with a friend named Julian. I remember it as if it were yesterday. This is how fresh the memory of God's faithfulness to me is. We were standing at the corner of North Main Street and Moffett Memorial Street in Danville, Virginia. Julian was a little older than I was, and he listened attentively as I told him that God had called me to preach and that I knew that He was also leading me to go to college to study for the ministry. Julian smiled as he listened and nodded in agreement. He asked what schools I was considering, and I began to list several of them.

Our Need and God's Provision

Finally, I stopped and said, "The problem is, I just don't have enough money. I can't go to college on the money I make delivering newspapers." I knew that God's promise to me and to each one of us is that nothing is impossible for Him. When He is involved and we are living life according to His will—that means surrendered to Him and His desires—then He will set up the circumstances of our lives so that we are fulfilling His plan. I continued to tell Julian that one particular college cost less, but it was not the one that I felt the Lord was leading me to attend.

As he listened, I noticed that he had lifted his eyes and was about to say hello to someone who was crossing the street and heading our way. It was the pastor of Moffett Memorial Baptist Church. Before I knew what was happening, Julian and I were wrapped in a conversation with this kind and considerate pastor. I had only been a member of his congregation for a short time. After a few minutes, Julian began to explain my situation to Reverend Hammock. He said, "Reverend Hammock, Charles believes God is calling him to preach, and he wants to go to school, but he doesn't have the money that is needed." Reverend Hammock already knew I was delivering papers because I was his paperboy!

Julian continued, "He needs some help. Is there any way we can help him?" The elder pastor looked at both of us, thought for a moment, and then said, "Charles, why don't you come to see me tomorrow?" I had no idea what this man would be able to do to help me, but I thought, *If he only commits to pray for me, then I know God will answer his prayers and provide the money that is needed.* The next day, I went to his study and sat down with him. Before I could say a word, he told me that he could get me a scholarship for the entire four years. I was amazed and left his office that day with a smile on my face and a heart full of praise to God.

Some people may think that this was a coincidence, but it was not. There was nothing coincidental about it. God set up the circumstances in my life, and He provided the answer I needed exactly when I needed it the most (Eph. 1:11). He has continued to work in my life in similar ways, and He will do the same for you. In God's eyes, each one of us is just as important as the next person. What God does for one person, He will do for everyone. His faithfulness is not limited.

The circumstances of your life are extremely important. Never ignore them because they are exactly what God uses to direct your life and to reveal His promise to you. When God is involved, it is never a matter of luck or good fortune. There is no such thing as luck in the life of a believer. It is the hand of God that opens and closes the doors you face each day. There is no chance encounter—

just the divine moments when God moves to answer your prayers and accomplish His purposes.

There are three things we need to know concerning God's promise.

He will show us His will. He desires that we know it and assumes responsibility for telling us how to live each day in the center of His will. This is a part of His nature and character. It is, however, our responsibility to do what He leads us to do. If He says move forward, as He did with Abraham and Peter, then we need to put on our walking shoes and move forward by faith, trusting Him to set up the circumstances of our life and to provide for the needs we have.

He is committed to our success. He wants us to live in the center of His will. This is why it is not a mystery that cannot be found or discovered. He tells us in Psalm 32, "I will instruct you and teach you in the way which you should go; I will counsel you with My eye upon you" (v. 8). From our birth, God has been working the circumstances of our lives together in order for us to fulfill His will. However, because we live in a fallen world, we often get off track. Yet God remains steadfast in His desire to teach us how to fulfill His purpose and plan for our lives. David knew God had a plan for his life, but he didn't know all the aspects of that plan.

However, he realized if he would commit himself to follow wherever the Lord led him, he would discover it. It would unfold before him over time, and this is exactly what happened. There are times when God places a dream or a goal in our hearts, and we have to step forward with the intent of reaching that goal. If we say, "Lord, I don't want to move until I can see the whole picture laid out before me," then we will miss not only a great blessing, but we also will miss His will for our lives.

He will correct and redirect us when we make a wrong turn. Many of the people that I talk with have made mistakes in their walk with the Lord. Maybe they made wrong choices that ended up devastating their families. Others have written to say that they felt God was leading them to a certain line of employment, and they ignored His call. Years later, they are fighting feelings of hopelessness as they wonder if it is too late for them to discover God's will for their lives, and the answer is no. His promise is the same as it was the day you were born. God doesn't change; we may, but He is the same yesterday, today, and forever.

No matter how badly you have messed up, He will take the broken pieces of your life and, with the glue of His unconditional love, put your life back together. Whenever you turn back to Him, seek His forgiveness, and ask Him to guide you from this point on, He is quick to embrace you with His unconditional love and forgiveness. He says, "I will take you, right where you are, and show you how to live out the rest of your life with My help and My strength."

A Crucial Discovery

One of the first things we need to learn is that God is a planner and not a reactor. He planned creation. He also planned for your life. He planned the birth of His Son, the Lord Jesus Christ, and He planned for His death so that we might have eternal life through faith in Him. He planned to establish His people through the local church. He also has planned a heavenly home for us so that we will never be separated from His eternal goodness, love, and mercy.

He has full knowledge of your life, and yet He designed you for a purpose just as He designed the men and women of the Bible for their purposes. For example, though Paul once persecuted the church and witnessed many believers being put to death, God chose the apostle Paul to preach the gospel throughout the known world.

On the Damascus Road, Christ spoke to Paul, and from that moment on, everything was different (Acts 9:1–19).

Paul's life took on a new meaning. Suddenly, Paul's life and everything attached to it was changed. Once he had been a critical, unbelieving person, but a few moments in the presence of the living Lord was all it took to change his eternal destiny and set him on a pathway that was perfectly in line with God's purpose for his life.

Maybe you can relate to Paul's story. He was older when he met the Lord and had formulated a distinct plan for his life. However, when Jesus Christ got ahold of his life, his response was immediately one of ultimate surrender. For years, he resisted becoming a Christian, and if he had said no to Christ, he would have missed an eternal blessing. Not only would he have missed God's will, he also would have missed the opportunity to be saved, to know God personally, and to be a part of the greatest mission effort this world has known.

What is holding you back from doing God's will? Most of us know when God calls to us. We can sense His presence drawing near because it is unlike anything we have known. However, if we ignore it, then God's signal to us grows a little weaker each time. Finally, it is barely audible in our spirits.

Often, people say no to the Lord without thinking about the serious consequences of their decision. They resist Him because of their fears and believe that there is no way they can do what He has given them to do. They have failed to grasp the truth and the reality of Matthew 19:26: "With people this is impossible, but with God all things are possible." Finding His will is not difficult, but it does require a deep desire to please the Lord and a heart that is devoted to Him.

Honor God with Your Life

Think about it for a minute. If we had known Paul before he was saved, we would say, "There is no way this man would ever preach the gospel." The fact was that Saul's life did not honor God in any way. However, he made a crucial discovery, and that was his need for a personal Savior. Before you can know God's will for your life, you must realize that He has a plan, and the only way you can fulfill it is to surrender your life to Him. Holding back a certain area prevents God from fully blessing you and revealing His will to you.

We may wonder, *Why did Jesus wait so long to save Paul? Why didn't He approach him while He was on the earth?* Timing is one of the most important aspects of knowing God. He has a perfect time for every event to take place. We may decide that we will go on vacation tomorrow, but God is the one who ultimately holds the reins to our lives in His loving hands. Our decisions are just that, ours. However, decisions that are in step with God's plan and purpose will bring glory and honor to Him. They also will bring tremendous blessings to our lives because we have committed ourselves to obeying Him.

Until Paul met the risen Christ, he was living a life of frustration and self-determination. Nothing is more exhausting than a life fueled by self-energy. If this is where you are in life, then you could be one step away from burnout. Not everyone believes this. Many people believe they can go through life and never worry about God's desire for them. However, if we think about it, from the first moment of creation, God was planning for our redemption. He chose Abraham, through whom Christ's genealogical line would come.

Life does not exist so we can think, *Well, I'll just do the best I can and get by some way.* God has a purpose in mind for your life, and when you operate within its guidelines, you will excel far beyond anything you could imagine. This is why Paul writes, "We have obtained an inheritance, having been predestined according to His purpose who works all things after the counsel of His will" (Eph. 1:11). Just as Jesus Christ is our Savior, we are His inheritance. God has an overarching plan for our eternity, but He also has a plan for our lives and the way we spend our days on this earth.

CHAPTER THREE
How Do We Discover God's Promise?

The last thing God wants us to do is to sit around passively hoping everything will work out or come together. Yet many people do just that; they wait for God to open a door, and they do little to seek His will concerning their situation. Others know that they are in a holding pattern; but instead of using this pause in life for prayer and praise for what God has done in the past, they get restless and, if they are not careful, can drift in their devotion to the Lord.

Waiting for God's timing requires patience and commitment. Even Joseph, as faithful as he was in his walk with the Lord, had to wait many years for God's plan to unfold in his life. As a young man, the Lord had given him a promise, but he did not see it being fulfilled, nor did it follow an expected course (Gen. 39–40).

Through a dream, God had revealed to Joseph that one day he would rule over his brothers. His immaturity led him to disclose the contents of his dream, and his brothers were jealous and furious. Therefore, they plotted his death and threw him into a pit where he was left to die. However, a group of Midianite traders pulled Joseph out of the pit, but not in order to save him. Instead, they sold him as a slave in the land of Egypt (Gen. 37:28). Years passed, and Joseph was forced to face many heartbreaking trials. He was abandoned, forgotten, rejected, and persecuted, but the Bible tells us that through all of this, God was with him (Gen. 39:3).

You may feel as though those around you have rejected you. Loneliness has eaten away at your heart, and it's hard to believe that God will ever use you, let alone have a promise for your life. Bitterness and a cynical attitude are growing within your heart. Joseph was alone, but he kept the focus of his life set on God's promise to him. The Bible says that even in prison, "The LORD was with Joseph, so he became a successful man" (Gen. 39:2). You may not see it because Satan has blinded you to the truth, but God has a promise and a will for your life. His desire is not one of destruction but one of hope, and one that will bring many blessings into your life. He tells us in Hebrews never to give up: "Let us hold fast the confession of our hope without wavering, for He who promised is faithful" (10:23).

Because God has a plan for your life, He can take even the most trying set of circumstances and mold and shape them so that you may fulfill His purpose. From our perspective, it may appear that we are way off course, but from God's vantage point, we are following His pathway. Just as He was with Joseph, He is with you and me.

How do we discover God's promise, which is His will and purpose for our lives? Through:

- reading His Word
- the circumstances of life
- godly counsel
- listening to your spirit-driven conscience

First, God reveals His will to us through His Word. The saints in the Bible learned to meditate on His Word and truth. They studied His principles and went over the facts concerning how He had worked in the lives of others. As we pray and study His Word, the Holy Spirit leads us to passages of Scripture that fit exactly with what God wants us to do or learn. The Bible is God's primary form of communication with us. We can't live the Christian life apart from God's Word. Once we begin to read it, we will want to continue. As we study its message, we will see God's hand guiding, teaching, and spiritually nurturing us so we will find the right road to travel.

God placed a love for His Word deep in my heart, but He also gave me a desire to teach the truth of His Word to others. My desire was not just to study God's Word for myself; I wanted to tell as many people as possible how they could experience true freedom, hope, and unconditional love through a personal relationship with God's Son. All of this is based on His Word and my desire to do His will. What is your deepest desire? Is it to know Jesus first? Or are you battling with feelings and desires that, if left unchecked, could lead you far from God's planned purpose for your life? If this is the case, stop right where you are and tell the Lord about the confusion you are feeling. Confusion is not from Him but from the enemy, whose greatest desire is to prevent you from accomplishing God's purpose for your life.

We were not placed on this earth simply for our own pleasure. God gave us life so that we could enjoy His fellowship and the fellowship of other believers. He desires our friendship and demands our worship. Far too often, however, we have left our posts and gone off to chase dreams and goals other than the ones God has given us.

My prayer is that He would become not only your Lord and Savior but also your purpose for living each day. Once this happens, you will know abundant joy and peace that cannot be shaken.

Second, God reveals His will and promises to us through the circumstances of life. There are times, from our natural perspective, that life may seem out of sorts. We may face a sudden tragedy or loss. Without warning, a husband or wife may come to us and say he or she is leaving. Maybe there were things that we should have done differently, but now it is too late. Our lives are shattered by our circumstances, and the stress feels unbelievable.

We wonder, *How can any good come out of such sorrow?* God never finds delight in our suffering. He is not glorified by evil or the brokenness of our world, but He certainly can do the impossible. What appears to be an ending is really a beginning to Him. Yes, He cares when we hurt. He cried at the tomb of His friend Lazarus, and His heart cries even now with us when we are hurting. However, just as Lazarus rose from the grave, God wants to resurrect our lives. We may go through a season of mourning, but it will not last forever (Ps. 30:5; 51:12). When we allow Him to move close to us, He will heal our hearts and shattered dreams and lead us on to a spacious place of blessing (Ps. 18:19).

God uses the circumstances of our lives to reveal His will to us. He also uses them to position us for a greater purpose and blessing. What seems to be a dead end to you today may be God's avenue of hope tomorrow. You need to be willing to stay on course and believe that He is using everything in your life to accomplish His will (Rom. 8:28). There may be times when we are tempted to wonder how we will reach the goals He has given us, but we will because He is guiding us through the circumstances of our lives. Every turn we take, every challenge we face, and every disappointment that works its way into our lives are opportunities for Him to demonstrate His faithfulness to us.

We may think that we are just going through a daily grind, but we are not. That so-called daily grind is leading us to a place and a position where God can bless us and use us in ways that we could never imagine. Every challenge we face is used by God to prepare us for the next step in life. We never stop growing, and He never stops working in our lives. Even to our dying day, God is working His will out through our lives. I've never lost sight of this fact, even when life became very difficult, and I wondered what in the world God was doing in my life. I knew that He had a plan, and my responsibility was to stay focused on Him, allow Him to guide me, and be willing to obey Him in every situation. If I did that, He would take care of the details, and the same is true for you.

Joseph's life was outlined by sorrow and tragedy. However, not a moment was wasted. Every hour and day that he spent in captivity was building a strength within him that could not be gained any other way. He was learning the deeper principles of God. The apostle Paul had a similar experience. He was arrested and placed in jail for doing the very thing that God had given him to do—preach the gospel. He could have easily become discouraged and thought, "God, why did You allow this to happen to me? I thought You had a plan for my life." But he didn't. Instead, he used the time he spent in jail to write some of the most important books in the Bible—Galatians, Ephesians, Philippians, and Colossians.

Joseph did not waste the time he spent in prison either. Though he had risen to a great position in Egypt only to be betrayed once again and thrown into jail, he kept a steadfast heart and became an entrusted prisoner. Once he was released, he was ready to be used by God. The promise that the Lord had made to him came to pass. Due to a famine in Jerusalem, his family ended up in Egypt under his care because God had elevated him to rule over all the land. He was second in power to Pharaoh.

Jeremiah 29:11–13 are verses that we can cling to, not only when we go through trials and heartache, but also when we know that we have taken a wrong turn and need God's mercy and grace. It is a promise that reaches out to us with boundless hope, "'For I know the plans that I have for you,' declares the LORD, 'plans for welfare and not for calamity to give you a future and a hope. Then you will call upon Me and come and pray to Me, and I will listen to you. You will seek Me and find Me when you search for Me with all your heart.'"

It is hard to stop reading at the end of the above verses. God goes on to say, "'I will be found by you,' declares the LORD, 'and I will restore your fortunes and will gather you from all the nations and from all the places where I have driven you,' declares the LORD, 'and I will bring you back to the place from where I sent you into exile'" (v. 14).

Even when we drift away from God's plan, He keeps His focus set on fulfilling His will in our lives. God never gives up on us. Until we draw our last breath, He is using the circumstances of life to position us to receive His love and countless blessings. Can we say no to God? Certainly, but once we have come to know Him as Savior and Lord, saying no becomes all too painful because our "no" places us on the outside of God's best for us.

The third way God reveals His promise for our life is through the godly counsel of others. Often, God speaks to us and reveals His will through the counsel of a godly friend, pastor, or counselor. In Proverbs, He reminds us, "Where there is no guidance the people fall, but in abundance of counselors there is victory" (11:14). However, we must always consider if what others say to us lines up with the Word of God.

Many well-meaning people have given counsel that is just not a part of God's plan for the other believer. Often, we see this in the lives of those who are single. They long to be married and openly express their desires. Loving Christians can push a man and woman into one another's lives without considering God's will.

After the vows have been said and the wedding music has ended, everyone goes home. The couple, however, must live together forever, and many times, this is when conflict arises. I remember one young man telling me that he had met who he was sure was the "girl of his dreams," and he was going to marry her. It seemed that his friends knew her and thought she was a perfect match for him. I asked him how long he had known her, and he said, "About a month."

I thought, *There is no way that a person can truly know someone in that short of a time frame.* I counseled him to give the relationship time to grow, but his mind was made up. They were married, and three months later, they were struggling with the decision they had made. Marriage is a commitment and not something we enter into lightly. Be sure when you have a decision to make that you openly seek God's desire. Remember, He has a plan for your life, and it could include the person you met only a month ago; but it would be a very wise decision on your part to take time to ask Him to make this clear through His Word and through the peace that you feel whenever you pray. Paul reminds the older women to instruct and offer guidance to the younger women (Titus 2:3). Regardless of the situation, the counsel we give and receive needs to be godly and something that we know God would approve. If we are unsure about a matter, we need to stop and wait for Him to lead us to the next step. He will, and He always does. Be patient, and be committed to receiving the best He has to offer for your life. That way, you will never be disappointed.

God reveals His will to us through our conscience. How do we know what is best? We know He has a planned will, but how can we be sure that we have discovered it? When we ask God to make His will plain to us, He will do it. He has placed within our lives a conscience, an awareness of His presence (Rom. 1:20). He trains our conscience with the principles written in His Word. This is why reading and studying the Bible is so crucial to our daily walk with God. If we have taken time to hide God's Word in our hearts, then we will have a clear and firm vision of the hope for the future.

When tragedy comes, we will stumble and grope for hope. However, if we have the principles of God within our hearts, we will know that when trouble comes, we are not alone. We will remember that His Holy Spirit who lives within us will never leave us alone. We will also recall the places in God's Word where He has promised to guide us and give us the wisdom we need to meet every challenge (Prov. 2:6; 9:10; 14:33).

The prophet Zephaniah tells us, "The LORD your God is in your midst, a victorious warrior. He will exult over you with joy, He will be quiet in His love, He will rejoice over you with shouts of joy" (3:17). The New International Version of the Bible puts it this way, "The LORD your God is with you, he is mighty to save. He will take great delight in you, he will quiet you with his love, he will rejoice over you with singing." God actually rejoices over us and loves us with an everlasting love. We don't have to cower in fear of what will happen tomorrow because God has gone out before us, and He has trodden the path that we will walk. This means that He has placed our enemies under His feet. We can walk victoriously through this life knowing that the God of the universe is with us, guiding our every step and leading us to places of hope and victory.

Why is it important to understand this truth? Because just as God has a plan for your life, Satan would like nothing better than to prevent you from achieving it. He not only wants to discourage the missionary who is faithfully serving the Lord around the world, but he also wants to discourage the person who is sitting right beside you in your office. His goal is to prevent every believer from reaching his or her full potential.

Once you have checked your course according to God's Word and have taken time to "seek His face" through prayer, you are ready to step forward. He will guide you in the way that you should go. This doesn't mean that you will never face difficulty. In fact, hardship and disappointment are tools that God uses to refine our lives and make His promise for us even brighter.

A Word of Caution

If a person is involved in a legalistic church, then he may have a hard time following his conscience. He knows what

God has told him in Scripture. He even can see how God's plan would include certain circumstances. However, his conscience is holding him back because he is afraid that the decision he makes will not be correct. This is because he has grown accustomed to being in an atmosphere where the pastor or a group of leaders tells the congregation, "You must do this, or you can't do that." Over time, members begin to think that if they displease the leaders of the church, then God will be displeased. This is a root cause for false guilt—guilt that is not from God.

False guilt creates feelings of anxiety and fear because no one can live up to a set of standards that has nothing to do with the Word of God. People have become paralyzed in their walk with God all because they feel too guilty to trust Him for something greater.

There is another side to this issue. We can become complacent and ignore the warnings of His Spirit. We may think God is leading in a certain direction, but we continue to face closed doors. There is a sense of restlessness in our spirits, and it is as though the Holy Spirit were saying, "Don't do it!" However, we continue to push forward anyway. True guilt is God's way of saying, "Hold it! What you are doing is wrong, and if you continue, you will have to bear the consequences of your disobedience."

While false guilt will cause anxiety, true guilt can lead to a greater sense of peace when we heed the warning and stop to listen for God's guidance. One woman told me that she was convinced God's will included the purchase of a new car. Financially, she was not in a position to support this decision. She prayed about it but really did not spend significant time in prayer. Later, she admitted that she had jumped to a conclusion because there was not anything preventing her from doing it. Many times, God watches to see how we will respond to a situation based on what we have learned in the past. She knew her resources were limited, but she did not listen to her conscience or stop when she felt uneasy in her spirit. Within six months of its purchase, the car had become a huge burden. She started pressuring her employer for a salary increase and complained to coworkers that she did not have enough money to carry her through the month.

Initially, God's warning is very loud, and we feel uncomfortable. However, if we continue to ignore it, we will hear it less and less until we cannot hear His words of caution at all. We are living in a moral climate that is devastating. People do all types of things and justify their actions as being perfectly fine. In fact, many believe that if they do not go along with the crowd, they will run the risk of being labeled socially and politically incorrect. If what others are doing is not in keeping with God's Word and principles, then it is better for us to follow God and not the ways of this world.

I would rather be standing in the middle of God's will, knowing that I am living my life to the best of my ability according to His principles, than living a lie and reaping the consequences of my sin. The apostle Paul tells us, "In later times some will fall away from the faith, paying attention to deceitful spirits and doctrines of demons, by means of the hypocrisy of liars seared in their own conscience as with a branding iron" (1 Tim. 4:1–2). He is not saying that these people will lose their salvation. Instead, he is saying that their consciences will be seared as if they had taken a hot iron and placed it on waxed paper. A seared conscience is deaf and blind to the things of God. Sadly, the person who is living with a seared conscience will miss the joy and the peace that come from intimately knowing God and doing His will.

God reveals His will to us through common sense. Once God has placed His principles in our hearts, He expects us to use our common sense to make wise decisions. We cannot do this apart from knowing His Word and applying it to our lives. Our common sense always should be filtered by the guidance of the Holy Spirit. For example, if a person is deeply in debt and struggling to pay his monthly bills, there is no way God would lead him to borrow even more money, increasing the amount he owes others. Common sense will never lead you in a direction that is contrary to God's will and principles. If your common sense is tuned to God's Word, it will shout a long and strong warning when you are headed in a wrong direction.

In Titus, Paul writes, "For the grace of God has appeared, bringing salvation to all men, instructing us to deny ungodliness and worldly desires and to live sensibly, righteously and godly in the present age" (2:11–12). Using common sense does not mean that we can do what we want to do. It is a gift of God just like the conscience that we use under the guidance of the Holy Spirit. If we use common sense, we won't drink, smoke, or use drugs.

On the other hand, our common sense will lead us to trust God in greater ways. I learned this truth years ago as a young man. Since that time, God has challenged my faith on several occasions through the ministry of In Touch. As we have grown, our ministry outreach has expanded. In the beginning, our staff was housed in one building; then we sensed that God was about to take us to another level. We needed to expand and build a separate building to house our radio and television equipment, studios, and personnel. However, we did not have the money for a major building project.

Our human reasoning told us the venture was impossible, but our common sense, which was directed by the Holy Spirit, led us to step forward by faith and trust God to provide for the need we had. Months into our planning, a man who had never donated to the ministry called and said that he could not shake the feeling that God wanted him to do something to help our ministry. He asked what we were doing and if we had any special needs.

I told him about our need of a building for the ministry. I also explained that I had found a building and the price was $2.7 million, but I thought I could buy it for $2 million. His response was, "I think I can handle that." A few days later, I received his check for the exact amount, and we were able to purchase the building and relocate our entire ministry to this property.

When we place our faith in God and take our hands off the problem, the need, the decision, or the relationship, He will work everything out according to His will for our lives in order to demonstrate His awesome power.

Why did the Lord lead us to step forward and begin planning for this project? The answer is simple: He wanted us to place our trust in Him and not in ourselves. If we had waited until we knew everything would work out perfectly and according to our plans, then we would have been acting in our own strength. Instead, we trusted the Lord for His provision and timing. God is our source for every need we have, in every situation we face.

When you are facing a difficult decision, trust Him to provide the wisdom you must have in order to continue toward your goal. You will never be disappointed by placing your faith in the One who holds the answer to every need you have.

CHAPTER FOUR
God's Will Defined

It is not unusual for a young man to come to me and say, "I'm really praying because I believe God may be calling me to preach, but I am not sure. I have been praying about this for some time. How can I know the will of God for my life? Is He calling me to preach or not?"

I always approach this subject carefully, but a good indication of God's will is a desire to move in a certain direction. Many times, I respond, "When you pray about this, if you sense Him leading you and motivating your interest in this area, then more than likely, you are on the right course. If He stirs your heart and there is an abiding compulsion in this direction, then this is probably what He has for you."

However, I also add that the way we know for sure that

God is leading us in a certain direction is by spending time with Him in prayer. The Lord gives us a strong desire to do His will. However, this does not mean that everyone will serve Him through being in the ministry. His promises are broad and cover every area of life. He may lead you to become a nurse, a college professor, or a high school football coach. No matter where you are or what profession you have, when your life is connected with His and you are committed to doing His will, then you will know how to live each day. The decisions you make will be in line with what God has planned because your life is surrendered to Him, and there is no way that He will not make His will very plain and evident to you.

Two Aspects to God's Will

There are two major aspects to the will of God. First, God has a *determined will*. Second, He has a *desired will*. The determined will is God's sovereign, operational will in the world. It reflects how God operates as the Lord of the universe. The Bible tells us that He has established His throne in the heavens, and His sovereignty rules over all (Ps. 11:4). The problem is that some people do not believe that He is in control of all things; but if He is not, then who is? Satan is not in control. He has limited abilities that God has allowed to be operational in the world, but he is not sovereign and certainly not in control of God's creation. Likewise, we are not in control of our world or our destinies. God is the only one who has His hand on the controls.

This world did not create itself. Mankind did not begin life as a result of the evolution from a single-celled animal. God created us in His image, and the light of His love lives within those who have placed their faith in His Son, the Lord Jesus Christ. What a marvelous gift we have been given by God—life and breath and enough joy to live each day without feelings of fear or anxiety. The reason? The One who created us watches over us and has promised never to leave us (John 14:16). That is sovereignty and absolute control.

God's determined will is what must be done in this world. It is not up for discussion, nor is it optional. This means that whatever falls within His determined will absolutely, inevitably will happen. His determined will is also immutable. This means it is not going to change. It is irresistible in the sense that no one can ignore it or decide that it will not take place. It also is unconditional. There are some things that God does and will do that only He understands.

His determined will is comprehensive and purposeful, as well as unpredictable. For example, in Ephesians the apostle Paul writes, "He predestined us to adoption as sons through Jesus Christ to Himself, according to the kind intention of His will, to the praise of the glory of His grace, which He freely bestowed on us in the Beloved" (1:5–6). In love, He predestined you to the adoption of His Son. This means He drew a circle around your life once you came to know Christ as your Lord and Savior.

Those who receive Jesus Christ as their personal Savior belong to Him forever. Once you have come to know the Lord as your Savior, you cannot lose your salvation. You may yield to temptation, fall into sin, and even walk away from God, but He never stops loving you. This does not mean that you will avoid His discipline or the consequences of sin. Often, He allows us to experience suffering so that He can gain our attention and motivate us to return to Him. David reminds us that we can never travel away from His presence. "Even before there is a word on my tongue, behold, O LORD, You know it all. You have enclosed me behind and before, and laid Your hand upon me. Such knowledge is too wonderful for me; it is too high, I cannot attain to it" (Ps. 139:4–6).

God Makes Known His Will

The knowledge of God is too great for us to know. We may gain knowledge, but apart from God, we really know very little. He holds the world and all of us in His hands. We may think the government is in control of the future, but it is not. God is the One who places men and women in power. He also is the One who removes them. Without a doubt, He knows exactly what is going to take place and when it will happen. He is aware of the problems in the Middle East, but He is just as concerned about what is going on in your daily life. He is omniscient—all-knowing—and all-powerful. He cares when you are hurting or struggling with a decision and wants to guide you through your difficulty.

Paul tells us God has "made known to us the mystery of His will, according to His kind intention [that is according to His good pleasure] which He purposed in [Christ]" (Eph. 1:9). There are a lot of mysteries to God's will—events in the past and those to come that we will not fully understand. There will be some things that He shows us and other things that we will not know. Our minds cannot comprehend all the ways of God, but we can use the things He has revealed to us to discern His purpose in many situations (Deut. 30:16; Acts 2:28).

There is a difference between God's determined will and His desired will. His *determined will* includes the things in this life that He is going to do regardless of how we respond. It is absolutely indisputable and irresistible. However, the same is not true of His *desired* will, which includes the things that He wants to do. His *determined* will happens outside our sphere of control. God says that a certain thing will happen, and it does. Period. This also includes the things that He will do regardless of our cooperation or not. His desired will includes the things that He wants to do. When it comes to His desired will, we have a choice. We can obey or disobey Him. Included in God's desired will are decisions that we make each day. They may be major or minor choices.

One of the reasons so many of God's people are not living in His will is because they do not understand it, and they get confused. They wobble through life, hoping that they are on the right pathway. His determined will is very clear-cut—Jesus came to save us from our sin. God's mercy and grace were demonstrated through His Son's life and death. Do we understand how Christ was conceived? We know it was by the power of the Holy Spirit, but God has not chosen to reveal every aspect to us.

The Step Before Us

When it comes to His desired will, He provides instruction so we will know what we need to do, but we must decide to follow His instruction. In Colossians, Paul writes, "For this reason also, since the day we heard of it, we have not ceased to pray for you and to ask that you may be filled with the knowledge of His will in all spiritual wisdom and understanding" (1:9). This was Paul's prayer for the Colossian church, and it really is God's prayer for each one of us so that we might know and experience His personal will for our lives.

In her book *Candles in the Dark*, Amy Carmichael writes, "If the next step is clear, then the one thing to do is to take it. . . . Once when I was climbing at night in the forest before there was a made path, I learned what the word meant in Psalm 119:105: 'Thy word is a light to my path.' I had a lantern and had to hold it very low or I should certainly have slipped on those rough rocks. We don't walk spiritually by electric light but by a hand lantern. And a lantern only shows the next step—not several ahead." When we walk with our eyes set on Christ, then we will do His will.

A life that is focused on obedience is a life that is lived in the center of God's will. One of the first things that trainers teach their animals, especially dogs, is to watch them. The command of "watch" is given, and the dog learns to stay focused only on its master. Even if there is noise or other activity, the animal must hold its watch. The only person who can break this command is the owner or trainer. The purpose is simple. When the animal is watching its master, it is not distracted.

On a greater scale, if the focus of our hearts is set on Christ, then when we have to make a decision, we will do several things:

- We will turn to the Lord in prayer.
- We will be willing to wait for His answer.
- We will take time to seek His wisdom through reading His Word.
- We will obey Him.

Trust God Above All Else

It all boils down to a level of trust. Do we trust God with our lives regardless of what we see, or is there a shadow of doubt lurking in the back of our minds? One second of doubt can change the way we view God's presence in our lives. For example, many people believe the Bible contains the Word of God. Here is the error: The Bible does not *just* contain God's Word to us; it *is* the Word of God. Period. The moment you say, "Well, I don't know if every single word written within it is true," is the moment you discredit what God has spoken to us through His Word.

The Bible totally relates to your life and situation right now. It is the infallible Word of God—written by God Himself, through men who were His agents or scribes. They were His chosen vessels to record His principles and plan of redemption for a lost and desperate world. If you deny even a part of God's Word, you take a major step in the wrong direction—a direction that leads far from God's will and purpose for your life. It is also a direction that leads along a pathway of doubt, fear, and anxiety. The results of a single decision as this one can bring more heartache and sorrow than you can bear, because apart from faith in God and His Word, you will begin to drift spiritually. You will lose your sense of direction because you have tossed aside the very compass God has given you to keep you on course and in the center of His will.

However, when we choose to obey the Lord, we are telling Him that we believe He is who He says He is. We have a choice to believe or not to believe. If we choose to obey and believe, we will come out a winner every time. It is foolish not to obey God.

I learned this principle years ago. I was preaching a revival in Alexandria, Virginia, when I began to feel God churning something up inside of me. I kept thinking, "God, I don't know what You are trying to say to me, but whatever it is, please show me."

After the Wednesday night service, I went back to my room and knew that God was calling me into a season of prayer. I wanted to know what God was doing in my life. Many times, when feelings like this come, I take out a legal pad and list what I am feeling or any impressions I have had that could be from God. This night, I drew a circle with five lines coming out from it. On each line, I wrote the following:

- Do something unusual in my life.
- Change me in some area of my life.
- Do something in my ministry.
- Move me.
- ?

I placed a question mark on the last line because there seemed to be more, but I was not sure what it was. Then

I prayed and waited, but nothing seemed to indicate that God was ready to reveal His plan to me. However, the next night as I got down on my knees to pray, I instantly knew that God was saying, "I'm going to move you."

Responding to God's Direction

My mind started to race, and I asked, "Lord, when?" Then it was as if a large screen appeared in my mind with the word *September* written on it. It was April, and immediately I thought, *He must mean next September because I have only been at here in Bartow, Florida, for eleven months.* The next night, I got down on my knees to pray, but it was as if God had disappeared. He had said exactly what He needed to say, and, for the moment, there was nothing else I needed to know.

I came home and told my family what had happened, and we prayed that God would make His will clear. The following Monday, a man whom I had not talked with for a very long time called. After a few minutes of general conversation, he began to tell me why he had called. My thoughts returned to the legal pad and the question mark I had placed on line five.

He wanted to talk with me about a position that was open at his church in Atlanta, Georgia. I was the senior pastor of the church in Florida, but this position was for an associate pastor. I told him that he could probably think of fifty people to recommend for that position. However, he replied that my name was the only one that kept coming to mind.

I assured him that I wouldn't be interested in becoming an associate pastor and besides, I told him, "I love it here in Bartow." Before we hung up, he asked me if I would be willing to pray about it, and I agreed to do this. Once I hung up the phone, I burst into tears because I thought, "Lord, what are You doing?"

A couple of weeks later, a pulpit committee from First Baptist Atlanta showed up at my church to hear me preach. I continued to assure them that I was not interested. Every week for the next several weeks, someone called to check to see if I had changed my mind, but my answer remained the same: No. Finally, they asked if they could return for another visit. While I hated to see them waste their time, I agreed. This time, eleven people came, as well as the senior pastor.

Throughout this process, I could not stop the inner churning that was going on inside of me. I listened as they explained their offer and desire to see me become their new associate pastor. When they had finished, the senior pastor asked, "What is your answer?" I said that God would have to make it so clear to me that there would be no mistake that this move was His will for my life.

The committee left, and I began to seek God's face for His will for my family and me. I had never really been to Atlanta and knew very little about the city. On the other hand, I loved the people of our church and enjoyed being so close to the ocean. The word *September* continued to pop up in my mind. In fact, I could not erase it from my thoughts, nor could I stop praying about the move to a new city, even though it would mean that I would not be a senior pastor.

No Other Answer

Finally, I realized in my spirit that there would be no rest or peace until I accepted the offer. After talking my decision through with my family, I called the pulpit committee at FBA and accepted its offer. The moment I did this, the churning stopped. A footnote to this story is that by September of that same year, my family had moved to Atlanta, and I was in my new position. God knew exactly what He wanted me to do, and He even revealed the time frame to me. While it was a decision that I did not want to make, it certainly is one that I have never regretted.

Years later, as senior pastor to a spiritually strong and growing congregation, I can say without hesitation, if God is leading you to do something, don't resist Him. Get on board with His plan for your life. You will never regret obeying Him. He is the only One who has all the facts, knows all the truth there is to know, and has a wonderful plan in mind for your life. Still the question remains, can we know the will of God? The answer is yes, but in a limited way.

While on earth, even Jesus did not know all that His heavenly Father knew about the future. When questioned about the hour of His return, Christ told His disciples, "That day or hour no one knows, not even the angels in heaven, nor the Son, but the Father alone" (Mark 13:32). While on the earth, there was a limitation to what Jesus knew. He was God in the flesh, but He also was human.

However, God has full knowledge now, and when we ask for His guidance in a particular situation, He will provide it (Ps. 73:24; Matt. 7:7). Never lose sight of the fact that God's determined will is just that—what He has determined will happen. Nothing can change it. One day, He will return for those who have placed their faith in Him. This is an upcoming event, and we can rest assured that it will take place. His goal for us is to prepare us for the day of His coming by leading and guiding us through His Spirit into truth and godly understanding.

In Psalm 25, David prays a prayer that we can pray each day: "Make me know Your ways, O LORD; teach me Your paths. Lead me in Your truth and teach me, for You are the God of my salvation" (vv. 4–5). If you really want to catch God's attention, ask Him to "teach you more about His ways" as He guides you each day. He will not resist a heart that is fully submitted to Him.

CHAPTER FIVE
A Miraculous Hope!

I f we can know what God wants us to do in a given situation, then what mystery is Paul talking about in the first chapter of Ephesians? Again, it is a portion of God's determined will that He reveals to us. His redemptive plan includes you and me. He planned for our salvation before the beginning of time even though He knew each one of us would choose to disobey Him.

However, through His marvelous grace, we are given the opportunity to experience salvation and a new life. Apart from the death and resurrection of Jesus Christ, we would be lost without a single hope. God's Son willingly took our place on the cross and bore our sins so that we might have a personal relationship with God.

The mystery that Paul uncovered is the fact that God

has included us in His family. Those who place their faith in His Son are grafted into His family. The Jews in Paul's day would not accept this fact. Paul almost lost his life preaching this message. However, because he did not waver in his obedience but continued to preach the gospel, we have this truth to live by each day. Not only are we in a position to enjoy the goodness of God's love for eternity, we can also live in the light of His eternal acceptance as His beloved children. John tells us that we have been set free from the bondage of sin and death (John 8:32–36).

There are many aspects of God's will that we must accept by faith. There is no way to explain all that He does or will do in the future. This is because He is God, and He is sovereign. He does not promise to give us total understanding. However, He promises that if we will obey and trust Him, we will be blessed no matter what comes our way. We may or may not understand all that happens. If we do not, our responsibility is to continue to obey Him. God sees the big picture. From His perspective, life is fitting together. Yet, at times, from our point of view, it may appear to be coming apart.

When many in her family were arrested and sentenced to a Nazi death camp, Christian author and speaker Corrie ten Boom could not understand what God was doing.

Her family had sheltered and helped many Jews to escape Poland, but now that she was arrested, who would help her? How could this possibly fit into God's plan for their lives? Yet no sooner had they arrived at their second destination than Corrie and her sister, Betsie, began telling others about the Savior's love.

In the book *Prison Letters*, she writes that God placed her "side-by-side with Communists, criminals, Jehovah's Witnesses, Christian Reformed, liberals, and prostitutes." These were just some of the people who began to attend her nightly Bible studies. After her release, she writes about the time she spent at one of the worst camps:

> During my confinement in Ravensbruck, where mail was nonexistent, I felt a great emptiness. This was compounded when Betsie became one of the 97,000 women to die there. When Betsie died in camp in the winter of 1944, she left this world with a smile on her face, the smile of one who knows the Savior. She was gone, but I knew she experienced the happiness of Eternity.
>
> The horrors of Ravensbruck, especially Betsie's death, caused me to wake up to reality. When I did, I was able to see that when all the securities of the world are falling away, then you realize, like never before,

what it means to have your security in Jesus. It was not until December 28, 1944, when, through a miracle, I was set free just a week before all the women my age and older were put to death. I was free and knew then, as I know now, it was my chance to take to the world God's message of the victory of Jesus Christ in the midst of the deepest evil of man. (© Baker Publishing Group 1975)

God's Plan for a Lifetime

After her release, Corrie traveled the world telling people about the love and forgiveness of Jesus Christ. She had discovered the will of God for her life through tragic circumstances. However, instead of giving up and sitting on the sidelines of life, she obeyed the Savior's call, and thousands of people heard God's truth through this brave and dedicated woman.

Many people stand at a crossroad and wonder which way they should go. Never count God out of your plans because He who holds the future also holds your hand. Like Corrie, when life takes an unexpected turn, you can refuse to become embittered or frustrated because God knows what is up ahead. He can see the sunshine even though, for the moment, you are called to walk through a dark valley. The mystery of God's will is that we have been positioned by His grace to know Him and to live each day for Him. This is His destined will that you will know Him and glorify Him (Eph. 1:12).

At six weeks old, Fanny Crosby lost her eyesight at the hands of a man who claimed to be a physician. The grave error left the family in shock and sorrow. However, years later, she wrote, "If this accident was a mistake and if perfect earthly sight were offered to me tomorrow, I would not accept it." From her viewpoint, God's will was perfect. During her lifetime, she wrote over nine thousand hymns and witnessed to thousands of people.

You may think that somehow God has made a mistake and failed to keep His promise to you. He hasn't. He has only just begun to work out His marvelous will for your life. In one of her most famous songs, Fanny Crosby wrote:

All the way my Savior leads me; What have I to ask beside?
Can I doubt His tender mercy, Who through life has been my guide?
Heavenly peace, divinest comfort, Here by faith in Him to dwell!

For I know whate'er befall me, Jesus doeth all things
well;
For I know whate'er befall me, Jesus doeth all things
well.

A Step Further

Paul takes God's promise of mankind's redemption a step further and tells us that we have been "sealed in [Christ] with the Holy Spirit of promise, who is given as a pledge of our inheritance, with a view to the redemption of God's own possession, to the praise of His glory" (Eph. 1:13–14). We have a promised inheritance through Jesus Christ that is eternal. The Holy Spirit has sealed those who have placed their faith in God's Son. We belong to Jesus Christ, and no one and nothing is strong enough to break this bond.

Life will hold many moments of joy and hope. It also will contain trials and difficulties that will test our faith in the One who has given us life abundantly. Instead of focusing on your circumstances, learn to watch for God's directive, and you will find a certain kind of peace for your heart and mind that is beyond anything this world knows.

Can God take your heartache, your trials and suffering, and even your sin and turn it into something good? Absolutely! Can He do this same thing on a worldwide basis? Yes. Is anything too difficult for God? No.

God's plan for mankind's redemption included the birth of a son to Abraham and Sarah. The problem was that Sarah was beyond childbearing age. In fact, she was at least ninety years old (Gen. 17:17). Sometimes God will allow us to wait for His will to unfold; but remember, we have said that God's determined or destined will cannot be changed. It will take place.

When Sarah overheard God repeat His promise of a son to her husband, she laughed, and the Lord asked Abraham, "Why did Sarah laugh, saying, 'Shall I indeed bear a child, when I am so old?'" (Gen. 18:13). Have you ever felt "caught" by God when you doubted His promise or instruction? Most of us have, and we also know what it feels like to quench His Spirit through a lack of faith in His ability.

God remained determined with Abraham, but He also revealed a portion of His loving nature and destined will to His servant when He said, "Is anything too difficult for the LORD? At the appointed time I will return to you, at this time next year, and Sarah will have a son" (Gen. 18:14). The Lord did not have to say another word to Abraham, but

He did. His grace is sufficient, and His love for us is long-suffering. Never give up. You never know just how close you are to fulfilling God's purposes for your life.

Three things can prevent us from stepping into the light of God's will:

Disobedience. Like Sarah, we get tired of waiting and forget what it feels like to live within the goodness of God's protective will. Instead of waiting, we want to rush ahead or go in another direction, and we suffer as the result of our decisions.

Setting the focus of our hearts on the things of this world. Remember, timing is everything to God. He has a set time for the events that will unfold in your life and in the future of our world. Fasting, if it is motivated by our own desires, will not change His mind. His clock is set to heaven's timetable, and we miss a blessing when we think we can convince God to move more quickly or change His mind.

Taking a shortcut around God's planned route. Not only did Sarah laugh at God's reminder of His promise to Abraham, but years before, she had taken matters into her own hands. The Middle East remains in turmoil today because of this one decision. Being convinced that God was not going to allow her to have a son, she recruited her maid to have one with her husband. Ishmael's birth set off a firestorm that is still blazing today.

Whenever you are tempted to doubt God's plan or timetable, stop and ask Him to speak to your heart and encourage you as you wait. Don't be afraid to ask Him to draw near to you. He wants you to finish the course that He has set before you. In fact, not only does He want you to finish, He wants you to become a victor in this life. When you set your heart on obeying Him and honoring Him with your life, this is exactly what you will do.

CHAPTER SIX

Hindrances to Discovering God's Promise

God calls some people to be pastors, missionaries, and Christian professionals. However, He calls most people to be teachers, engineers, homemakers, doctors, bankers, investors, crane operators, communication advisers, sales associates, technicians, artists, and much more. He gives people gifts, talents, and skills with the sole desire for them to glorify Him and to accomplish His purpose and plan for their lives. Think about this for a moment: where would we be without engineers? We would not have cars, airplanes, trains, or ships, and all of us would be walking. The general rule here is that God has a purpose for your life, and it may be in a profession that is not related to work in the ministry. However, He certainly leads us to be involved in our churches as teachers, ushers, musicians, choir members, committee members, and more.

Regardless of what God has gifted you to do, He also wants you to be aware of the hindrances to fulfilling His will. At some point, you will be tempted to leave your post of service and follow another road than the one He has planned for you to travel. If you are aware of the pitfalls, you will know in advance how to handle thoughts of drifting, disobedience, and ignoring what you know God wants you to do. In Psalm 90:12, we are reminded to pray, "[Father], teach us to number our days, that we may present to You a heart of wisdom."

The Danger of Drifting

Once while my family was vacationing in Florida, my son, Andy, and I decided to take a couple of inflatable rafts out into the ocean. We had lived near the beach long enough to understand how dangerous ocean currents could be. Before heading out, we placed two markers on the beach just in case we began to drift. We surmised that we could look up and see exactly where we needed to be. We set boundaries, and we knew that if we passed either one of these, we could end up going much farther down the beach than we planned.

Sure enough, as soon as we climbed on our rafts, we began to drift rapidly past one of the markers. Without hesitation, we dove back into the water and swam with our rafts back within the boundaries. This happened several times, and finally, we realized the current was just too strong, and we needed to get out of the water.

God sets boundaries for our lives (Job 26:10). These are meant to keep us in the center of His will. However, if we choose to ignore them, we could end up drifting away from His plan and purpose. Drifting in our devotion to God is very dangerous. It short-circuits His plans for us and prevents us from enjoying the goodness of His blessing. However, the closer we are to Him, the easier it is to do what He has called us to do; but many people fail to do this and sail off in a direction that is opposite from God's design.

Plenty of people say with a sigh, "I can't figure out why things don't work out for me." If this reflects what you are feeling, then take time to be alone with the Lord in prayer. Ask Him to reveal His will for your life or even for a certain situation. He wants you to learn how to discover what He has for you, and when you do, you will not be disappointed.

"The secret things belong to the LORD our God, but the things revealed belong to us and to our sons forever" (Deut. 29:29). While there are many things about this life that we will never know or understand—some things are just reserved for the mind of God—there is so much that God wants us to know and understand. However, we cannot tap into these until we have learned to seek God's will for our lives. This means being willing to focus on Him and not just a quick answer or a simple reply.

Some people believe their lives are so far off course that there is no way they can understand what God has for them. They struggle with feelings of inadequacy and wonder if He is pleased or angry with them. This is a very frustrating place to be because God wants each one of us to know that He loves us with an everlasting love. His emotions are never directed toward us in anger. We can grieve His Spirit to a point where He becomes very silent and allows the consequence of our sin to entrap us, but He will never stop loving us. He created each one of us for a purpose, and His goal is for us to live lives that will glorify and honor Him.

Whenever I hear a person expressing frustration and fear over not knowing what to do next, I stop him and tell him that the reason he is feeling this way is because he is not plugged into God's will. Or maybe he was, and he began to drift in his spiritual devotion to Christ. Doubts, misbeliefs, listening to those who are not living within the will of God, and many other things can work like a fast-moving undercurrent to pull us off course and away from God's plan. Perhaps it is time for you to get off the raft and swim to shore where you can once again have both feet on solid ground.

The Danger of Disobeying God

Just as deadly as drifting in our devotion to God is deciding to disobey what we know He wants us to do. There is rarely a day that goes by that we are not challenged to obey God and surrender to His will. A man I counseled had been married before, and he was about to file divorce papers for the second time. Though I knew that he was making a grave mistake, I also realized any words of counsel spoken to him would simply fall on deaf ears because wife number three was waiting in the wings. A move in the direction of another marriage would only help to dig a deeper emotional hole for him. After I explained how God's will for him did not include another divorce and marriage, he looked at me and said, "But I believe this new relationship is God's best." His answer was disheartening because I knew he was about to drift into dangerous waters. Disobedience always leads us away from God's will.

Most of us would hear a story like this and wonder how a person could miss seeing God's will. However, each day, numerous people make similar mistakes, and the consequences of their decisions are painful and devastating. God does not want us to have to face the brokenness that comes with divorce. However, people get involved in relationships all the time that should be avoided. They ignore the fact that disobedience builds a wall between God and us. It sidelines us from doing His will and leaves us in a narrow place where we struggle to find enough hope to continue each day.

The woman at the well is a prime example of a life that had been broken by sin, but God still had a plan and a purpose for her to fulfill. Obviously, she had searched for true love and not found it. She had been married several times and was living with a man who was not her husband. From her perspective, her life was at a dead end. Her reputation was so scarred that she could not even go to draw water at the local well with the other women. The words of imagined gossip flooded her mind, and she went alone to the well during the middle of the day. No one but those trapped deeply in sin ventured out in such heat. However, the Savior knew of her misery and the cry for freedom that lay buried deep within her heart.

Maybe you can identify with this woman's story. For years, you have lived life entrapped by sin and its consequences. You have ended up going through one relationship after another, and the person you are now involved with has no intention of marrying you. You feel defeated and find it hard to believe that God would have created you, let alone have a purpose for your life. In fact, you wonder if you prayed to Him, would He even hear your prayers? The answer is yes.

God never turns away from those who seek Him. He loves us with an everlasting love. The woman at the well was a seeker. She knew that her father and his father had worshipped God at a certain place (John 4:20). Jesus, however, knew a great deal more about her. He perceived her need for salvation, acceptance, forgiveness, and, most of all, unconditional love. This is what God offers everyone who comes to Him. We may think that our sins are too many or too dark to be forgiven, but nothing is more powerful than God's unconditional love. He knows your past, present, and future, and He will not reject you. Instead, He offers you an eternal hope that cannot be dashed.

He is willing to forgive and restore us. Jesus asked this woman for a drink of water, but this was just a way for Him to begin the conversation. He knew she was the one who needed the eternal water that only He could provide. She had been thirsty for a long time. Nothing she acquired could satisfy the need within her life. God is the only one who can meet the needs that we have. He created us and, in doing so, placed a need within our lives that only He could fill. It didn't matter how many pots this woman brought to the well. Until she met the Savior and drank from the cup of His eternal love, her life would remain parched and dry.

He always sets us on a pathway to hope. Jesus does not leave us comfortless (2 Cor. 1:3–4). The woman said to Jesus, "I know that Messiah is coming (He who is called Christ); when that One comes, He will declare all things to us" (John 4:25). We can imagine the Savior looking at the woman deeply as He said, "I am the one who is speaking to you" (v. 26). When she heard the Savior's words, her heart probably skipped, and she could not believe what she was hearing.

The Savior, the Messiah, the same God who had counseled Moses and Joshua and Daniel was talking with her—a sinner. Suddenly, the disciples stepped onto the scene and, after giving the woman a stern look, turned to Jesus. The woman, however, left their presence and headed straight into the city where she began to tell everyone what she had heard and discovered. "Many of the Samaritans believed in Him because of the word of the woman who testified, 'He told me all the things that I have done'" (John 4:39).

At times, you may be tempted to think that your life is without hope. This is never the case. God wants you to realize the problem of sin, the consequences of sin, and the sorrow that comes when we disobey God. Ask Him to open your eyes to the truth of your circumstances and be willing to turn away from any and every sin that He brings to mind. Then ask Him to restore you and to place you in a fellowship of believers and a Bible-believing church where you can grow spiritually. Never forget that God created you by His design for a specific purpose. An entire town was saved because of the testimony of one woman whose life was changed through an encounter with the Savior, and yours will be, too.

The Danger of Pride

It was pride that caused Satan's fall in heaven. God had created him and given him a countenance like no other creature. He was beautiful and was the one whom God called to lead worship in heaven, but this position of honor was not good enough. Instead of worshipping the Lord, Satan wanted to be worshipped. Instead of honoring God with his being, he wanted to be honored; instead of submitting to God's authority, he wanted to rule, and rule he has. However, he is not ruler over an eternal kingdom; he is the leader of a doomed régime—one that will see its future destruction in the Lake of Fire (Rev. 20:14).

Pride was the stroke of temptation that the enemy used in the garden of Eden to lure Eve into questioning and disobeying God. The Lord had given Adam and Eve certain guidelines, but they decided to take matters into their own hands by doing what God had told them not to do. They rebelled against God and suffered the serious consequences of their sins. The same is true for us today. The enemy tempts us with words that question God's goodness to us, or with thoughts that cause us to believe we have not received all that should be ours.

Pride is the opposite of humility and is opposed to the things of God. Judas decided that he knew better than Jesus. His thinking was very logical but very wrong and not in keeping with God's plan. We can do the same thing in our lives. God had a purpose for His Son's dying on the cross. However, Judas wanted Him not to die but to begin an earthly kingdom—one that would include him and the other disciples. His vision was earthbound and limited, and ours can be also.

In a moment of selfish pride, he betrayed the Messiah. Every act of sin is an act of rebellion against God, and it all comes from our desire to lead and not to follow. Pride is a very destructive force. It can lead to personal ruin and deep loneliness. However, you can stop it and prevent it from having easy access to your life. Ask God to reveal to you any pride that you may have in your life.

When Jesus told the disciples that He would be arrested and killed, Peter hastened to stop the Savior from saying more, "God forbid it, Lord! This shall never happen to You" (Matt. 16:22). The enemy's invitation of pride always contains a personal hook—one that is both selfish and not God's best for you.

Jesus countered Peter's statement with a powerful reminder, "Get behind Me, Satan! You are a stumbling block to Me; for you are not setting your mind on God's interests, but man's" (Matt. 16:23). The enemy's ploy always appeals to our flesh and our human nature. However, you do not have to fall for his tactics, nor do you have to settle for a life that is both prideful and isolated from

God's goodness and blessing. Seek what God has for you first and then all the desires of your heart will be fulfilled. Not only will you spend your days walking in the center of His will, your heart will be at rest because your life is surrendered to the One who has only your best in mind.

The Danger of Ignoring God's Will

When we think of God's will for our lives, we usually think on a very grand scale—something that is life-changing and eternal. However, while the Lord may not have a preference when it comes to what color of tie or shirt we wear for the day, He certainly is interested in every aspect of our lives. He wants us to look our best, do our best, and live in the light of His joy and hope. God also wants us to learn how to listen for His instruction even in times when we mistakenly believe our situation is small and insignificant.

I remember once waking up around 1:00 a.m. on a Saturday morning and realizing that I was very sick with a cold. I knew if I did not act quickly, I would not be able to preach on Sunday. As I lay in my bed praying, I sensed the Lord telling me to get up and get some chicken soup. The urge was so strong that I finally got up, went downstairs to the kitchen, and began searching through the cabinets to see if there was a can of chicken soup, but there wasn't.

"God, show me what to do because I can't call the doctor at this hour, and there is no chicken soup in the house." I was feeling worse with every passing minute. Suddenly, I sensed God saying, "Where do you get a can of chicken soup?"

I knew the answer—at the grocery store. However, that was not an exciting thought at that hour of the morning, especially feeling the way I did. But I knew better than to resist the Lord, so I got ready and drove to the store. God's will is not limited to the major matters of our lives. He is interested in all that concerns us. He wanted me to preach on Sunday, and He also had a plan for my sickness. He would use it to remind me that He was in total control of my life. If I would obey Him, He would give me the strength I needed to preach that weekend.

With this in mind, I drove to the store and bought three cans of chicken soup. I heated a large can, ate all of it, and then went back to bed. As I lay there talking to the Lord, I began to feel better and soon was fast asleep. In the morning, I woke up to a prompting of God's Spirit telling me that the chicken soup had gotten me through the night, but it was not going to heal me. I knew I needed to call the doctor. It is okay to have a cold or sinus problem on Monday, but not on Saturday when I was preparing for Sunday.

By 10:30 Saturday morning, I was sitting in my doctor's office. The next day was Sunday, and I was able to preach—in part because of the medicine the doctor prescribed, but mainly because God intervened, and I obeyed His instruction. If I had disregarded God's word to me, I never would have made it to church on Sunday. Though He wants us to think sensibly, He places thoughts in our minds that, if we follow them, will keep us centered in His will.

Likewise, Satan can do the same thing. He places ideas in our minds that are contrary to God's plan for us, and if we are not careful, we will end up following him. He will tell us things like, "Here is an opportunity for you to make a lot of money in a hurry," and we believe him. We avoid trouble by taking time to be sensitive to the words we hear and by praying and laying the idea out before the Lord. Ask God to show you who is doing the talking. If it is the Spirit of God, then His words always will glorify the Lord and never contradict His will for our lives or His Word.

The Danger of Living Separate from God's Peace

Some people have lived in an atmosphere of stress for so long, they cannot remember what it feels like to be encapsulated with a sense of God's peace. Feelings of anxiety invade their thoughts, and they cannot conceive how they will make it from day to day. However, peace is a gift that God gives each one of us. He tells us to "be anxious for nothing, but in everything by prayer and supplication with thanksgiving let your requests be made known to God. And the peace of God, which surpasses all comprehension, will guard your hearts and your minds in Christ Jesus" (Phil. 4:6–7).

In Colossians, Paul writes, "Let the peace of Christ rule in your hearts, to which you were called in one body; and be thankful" (3:15). Peace is God's umpire. When we have a true sense of peace within, then we know that what we are doing is right in the center of His will. If there is a lack of peace, stop and take time to pray and ask God to confirm His will for your life and situation. Sometimes you may need to take a step of faith, and then the peace will follow. In fact, the psalmist writes, "Cast your burden upon the LORD and He will sustain you; He will never allow the righteous to be shaken" (Ps. 55:22). God's presence in our lives is our sustaining peace (1 Pet. 5:7).

There will be other times when sorrow or trouble will come, and we will think, "Lord, what am I going to do?" The moment we turn to Him in prayer, a wonderful sense of peace floods our hearts. We don't know how we'll get through the upcoming days or months. However, because of His abiding presence, we are able not only to get through the difficulty, but go on to receive His victory.

CHAPTER SEVEN
Equipped for Every Good Work

No matter what we face in this life—sorrow, heartache, joy, or times of love and laughter with friends and family, God has a plan for it to be used in our lives. We were created to have an eternal mind-set. However, before we see this unfold, we must develop our personal relationship with Jesus Christ. I have heard many Christians tell how they could not understand God's will. Many say, "I wish I had understood what God wanted me to do in this situation or how He wanted me to respond. I feel as though I have missed something that He had for me." Usually, this statement was coupled with a story of regret, tragedy, sorrow, or loss.

We can know how to face life's challenges because God provides the wisdom we need at every turn. Also, we can learn to set goals for our lives based on His will and purpose. Neither one of these is hidden from us, but we must be willing to take the needed time to discover them through prayer, reading and studying His Word, and, if necessary, waiting for His timing.

While we may not understand all the reasons God allows a certain incident to happen or leads us to do a certain thing, we can know that He is at work in our lives. No matter what the circumstances may be, His goal is to draw us closer to Him and position us for blessing by fulfilling His will for our lives.

Bracing for a Strong Wind

What looks like tragedy to us will, over time, become a tool in God's hands to shape our lives so that we will be more sensitive to His Spirit and to the needs of others. However, one thing we cannot disregard in the process of understanding His will is God's Word. If we ignore the wisdom that it offers, then we will suffer the consequences of making unwise decisions.

The author of Hebrews writes, "Now the God of peace, who brought up from the dead the great Shepherd of the sheep through the blood of the eternal covenant, even Jesus our Lord, equip you in every good thing to do His will, working in us that which is pleasing in His sight, through Jesus Christ to whom be the glory forever and ever" (13:20–21). God is equipping us to be able to walk with Him on a daily basis and to do the things that are pleasing and honorable to Him. He is also preparing us to do mighty things for Him.

Reading and studying His Word is crucial to our spiritual growth. There is a tremendous amount of peace gained through knowing and even memorizing Scripture. When trouble comes, the Spirit will quicken a verse of Scripture to our minds. Or perhaps when we just need to be reminded of God's unconditional love for us, He will bring to mind a verse that is personal to us and to our relationship with the Savior. He encourages us the same way.

You may be praying about a certain need and just don't know which way to turn. Then you remember a certain portion of His Word and think just how much that means to you as you deal with your current circumstances. You didn't just "happen" to remember this Scripture; the Holy Spirit brought it to mind so that you would be encouraged and would keep walking in the correct direction. However, if you live life through the eyes of your own human reasoning, you will not experience a deep inner peace because you will always wonder, *Am I on the right track? Am I living in God's will?*

Storms will come and winds will blow hard against your life, but when the entirety of your life is wrapped up in Jesus Christ, you will feel little more than the push of a gentle wind. However, far too often, when tragedy strikes, we will cry out, wondering if God sees or understands our plight. He does, but He may be waiting to see if we will trust Him or cower in fear. He also wants us to learn that He is in full control of the circumstances surrounding our lives.

Over to the Other Side

The disciples learned this lesson out on the open Sea of Galilee, which is known for its sudden outbreak of storms and high winds. After a long day of teaching, Jesus instructed His disciples to get into a fishing boat and go to the other side of the lake (Mark 4:35). God had a plan in mind even for this venture. Christ's followers could have caught on to the fact that they would not die along the way because the Son of God already had said, "Let us go over to the other side." But they apparently missed this part of the discussion. When the wind started to pick up, they realized a storm was approaching.

Most of the men on board the boat were seasoned

fishermen. Peter, John, and James especially should have known how to deal with this type of weather, but the storm that hit their boat was so fierce that they were frightened beyond anything they had experienced. They began to cry out. Jesus, however, was in the stern of the boat lying on a cushion sound asleep. The promises of God lived within His heart, and He was not afraid. His followers had the Son of God with them—the promise of eternal hope and salvation—and yet they did not grasp this fact and became overwhelmed by fear.

Finally, one of them woke Him and said, "Teacher, do You not care that we are perishing?" (Mark 4:38). What a question to ask the Savior, the One who already had said, "We're going over to the other side."

Are you traveling through a difficult time in your life and wondering if you will survive? These men did, but you don't have to wonder or ask, "Lord, do You care?" He cares with an eternal love—one that has protected you and watched over you all of your life. When difficulties come, when you don't know the right decision to make at home or in your work, you can turn to the one Person who has given you a promise and knows that you will make it over "to the other side."

Jesus stood up and, more than likely, took a moment to

take stock of His bewildered team of frightened disciples. Then with all the power and force of heaven at His disposal, He rebuked the wind and said to the sea, "Hush, be still." Mark tells us that the "wind died down" and the sea became "perfectly calm" (4:35–39). Then Jesus turned to them and asked, "Why are you afraid? Do you still have no faith?" (v. 40).

Faith in God Is the Key

One of the requirements of discovering God's will is faith. It takes faith to uncover what He has planned for you to do. It also takes faith to hold the right course when the winds of adversity blow hard against your heart and mind. This is why it is so important to know God's Word and to pray, asking for His guidance each day. If the disciples had taken time to think clearly, they would have realized that they were in the company of the Savior, and He was not about to abandon them or His plan for their lives. Be encouraged when difficulty comes, because either you are on the right path or God is in the process of making a course correction in your life. Either way, when you submit your heart and life to Him, you will continue to advance and come away with a great blessing.

Many wonder how God can be glorified through the tragedies of life. If we truly trust Him, He will provide the peace and understanding we need to settle this issue. We live in a fallen world where bad things happen. However, God is infinitely good, and He has the ability to use our brokenness and sorrow for His glory and for our good.

The apostle Paul writes, "We know that God causes all things to work together for good to those who love God, to those who are called according to His purpose" (Rom. 8:28). God works all things together for good, but there is a condition to this promise, and it is this: We must live our lives devoted to Him. He loves us with an everlasting love, but He also desires our devotion and love in return. The will of God is wrapped up in our relationship to a loving God, who has only the very best in mind for each one of us.

When our world seems to fall apart, He is near to our hearts holding the eternal glue that prevents us from caving into hopelessness and sorrow. Certainly we can live life in a way that overcomes any obstacle because of His power within us. But what happens when we are living outside the will of God—when we have turned our backs to His plan and purpose? Two things that become very apparent are our lack of joy and lack of spiritual discernment.

"The golden rule for understanding spiritually," writes

Oswald Chambers in *My Utmost for His Highest*, "is not intellect but obedience. If a man wants scientific knowledge, intellectual curiosity is his guide; but if he wants insight into what Jesus Christ teaches, he can only get it by obedience."

Chambers goes on to write, "If things are dark to me, then I may be sure there is something I will not do. Intellectual darkness comes through ignorance; spiritual darkness comes because of something I do not intend to obey." Obedience is a key to finding God's will for your life. The moment you say, "No, Lord, I won't do that" is the moment that you miss out on a tremendous blessing because you have taken a step away from His will and one toward disobedience.

God's Glory—Our Good

It is easy to overlook the awesomeness of God's grace, especially for a person who has spent a life battling sin or some addiction. The person involved may not be able to conceive how God could love him, let alone have a plan for his life; but He does. From His perspective, there are no hopeless causes. The wonderful truth about God is that He loves us. Period. In fact, He loves us so much that He sent His Son to die for our sins. You may feel discouraged and as if you have wasted your life, but let me assure you that you have not. Even at the age of sixty-five or seventy-five or even older, God wants you to know that He loves you and still has a plan for your life. Though you may have spent years separated from Him, the moment you return or ask Him to save you, He does, and your new life in Christ begins.

You may be thinking, *Can God really be glorified through sin and disobedience?* The answer is yes. He doesn't want us to spend our lives entrapped or enslaved by sin. However, when we do yield to temptation and disobey Him, He will not remove His love from us. He created us with a design and plan in mind, but in order for this to take shape, we have to decide to yield our lives to Him. Once we do, He will position us to know a portion of His plan. We take one step and then He leads us on to another. Step by step, we follow the Savior to a place of blessing, hope, and inner peace (Ps. 29:11). We are never too old or too young to begin this process. The prodigal son made a horrendous mistake, but his father did not abandon his love for his son. Though he was sure he could live a life apart from the comforts of his father's home, he soon discovered just how wrong and foolish he was. However, this did not happen before he asked his father for his entire inheritance. Once he received it, he headed for the city where he promptly began to waste it by living a lifestyle that was destined for one ending: sorrow and heartache.

After the money was gone, the son quickly realized what he had done and how he had fallen prey to his own selfish desires. He was not living his fantasy; he was living a nightmare! Suddenly, he knew he had no place to turn. The only job that he could find was one of feeding pigs. After days of filling pig troughs with food that was better than what he had to eat, he came to his senses and decided to return to his father's house. He thought if he could be a servant, he would be better off doing that. We must realize that, as long as he was living outside of God's will, the blessings he once knew were cut off. However, once he gained a servant's heart and mind-set, the blessings returned and increased.

Nothing to Gain Apart from God

There is nothing to gain living apart from God's will. We certainly can't humanly discern His plan, and on our own, we become lost and very lonely even if we are in a crowd of people. In fact, you can have dozens of friends, but if there is a wall between you and the heart of God, then you are going to feel lonely and, more than likely, depressed. This young man's display of humility and confession brought glory to God. Did he step out of God's will? Yes, but God provided a way for him to experience complete restoration. Jesus told this story with one goal in mind: All of us, no matter what we have done or where we have been, can come home to our heavenly Father. There is no place you can travel that is too far from His love.

You can read the full story in Luke 15. However, the part people seem to enjoy the most is when the father races out to meet his returning son. Perhaps it is because all of us, at some point, have longed for the Lord to race out to meet us. We have all failed and sought His forgiveness and restoration. This young man probably thought for certain that he would be scolded and forced to live in the quarters set aside for those who worked for the family. Instead, the father called for the best robe to be put on his son and then for a "fatted" calf to be killed and cooked in honor of his son's return. Sin has consequences. Without a doubt, stepping out of God's will and away from His plan will bring heartache and regret. However, the moment you turn back to Him and say, "Lord, I was wrong. Can I come home?", He rushes out to meet you and gathers you up in His loving arms. The valley you walked through may have seemed tremendously dark. However, it was necessary to accomplish His loving will in your life. Even though you wondered if you would come out on the other side, God knew you would. He also knew that He would be waiting for you and would rush out to meet you and to tell you that He loves you.

Someone may say, "Well, is it okay to sin so God is glorified?" The answer is no. God wants us to live lives that are holy and pure before Him. He tells us to be holy because He is holy (Lev. 11:44). However, when we do sin, He has a plan in mind for our restoration—one that will ultimately lead us back to Him.

An Infinite Promise

Remember, He has promised that He will never leave us. It may appear that we have left Him, but we are never really out of His sight—just out of His will. Sooner or later, our actions will catch up with us, and when they do, we must decide whether to return home or keep running. There are people who run away from God their entire lives. Exhausted and full of anxiety, they no longer remember what decision led them away from their first love, the Lord

Jesus Christ. All they know is that running keeps them from thinking about tomorrow and the day after that.

One step of obedience stops the racing of our hearts. We may have to face the consequences of our decisions, but we can come home. When we do, a deep, abiding peace returns, and we know that we are, once again, walking in the center of His will. The best part of our restoration is that He puts us to work. Waiting around with nothing to do can breed feelings of insecurity, depression, and fear. The first thing the woman at the well did was to go into the city and tell people about the Savior. "The woman left her waterpot, and went into the city and said to the men, 'Come, see a man who told me all the things that I have done; this is not the Christ, is it?'" (John 4:28–29). The New International Version of the Bible records the last part of that sentence this way, "Could this be the Christ?" When news spread concerning Jesus, most of the town hurried out to meet Him. John records, "Many of the Samaritans believed in Him because of the word of the woman who testified" (John 4:39). God's will is for us to point people to His Son. The moment we turn to Him and acknowledge our need for Him, He meets the needs of our hearts.

He also places us in a position where we can tell others about His saving grace and matchless love. How can we do this? Just like this woman, we have experienced it firsthand; and while sin is never a good option for a believer, when we fall into its grasp and then step away from it, God is determined to restore us, give us hope, and set us on a road to service in His kingdom. To know and understand the will of God, you must come to a point where you realize that from God's perspective, there are no hopeless causes—no one beyond the reach of His infinite love. We can choose to deny Him, but He will never stop loving us.

Saying No to Temptation

Satan is the one who enjoys bringing destruction to our lives through the temptation of sin. He longs to lead us to a distant country by telling us that there is a better way to live than the one that God has planned for us. This is exactly what he did in the garden of Eden, and it is portrayed in the story of the prodigal son. The enemy tempted Adam and Eve to question God's authority and will for their lives. They believed his lie and ended up losing their home and place in paradise.

However, God had a plan. He knew the decision they would make. As He walked through the garden that evening looking for them, they really were not hidden from His sight. At that moment, His determined will for mankind's redemption began to fall into place. He provided clothing for them by slaying the first animal. This one act set into motion the coming of Christ hundreds of years later. It foreshadowed His sacrificial death for you and me. We never have to question God's goodness to us because, at every turn in our lives, He is present, leading, guiding, and providing for us.

You may be thinking, *I can never know God's will. It just seems overwhelming and impossible.* You can. The woman at the well stopped and listened to the Savior. She was right where she needed to be. From that moment on, her life changed dramatically. Suddenly she had a purpose. She could open her heart up to the dreams that God had for her. For years, she had been in bondage, and now she was free to really love and be loved. For the first time in her life, she was not struggling to be anything other than what God made her to be.

CHAPTER EIGHT
God's Will
Is Clear

I n order to experience this level of freedom and peace, we have to learn to be sensitive to His presence and listen to His word spoken to us. When my children were young, they often wanted to know what I thought they should do in certain situations. I remember being in my study one day and looking up to see both of them standing in the doorway. It was obvious that they wanted to ask me a question. Finally, one of them told me what they wanted to do and asked my opinion. I knew what was right, but I wanted to see what they would do; so I told them that they should pray about it and see what God had to say.

They both chimed in and said, "Aw, Dad, you always say that. We want to know what you think we should do." For a moment, I was tempted to answer their question but decided against it. God wants us to learn how to seek His wisdom for our lives—no matter how young or old we are. The easiest thing for me to do would have been to say no, or yes, or even maybe, but I wanted them to learn that they could go to God, and He would provide the right answer. One of the most important things parents can do is to teach their children to spend time with God asking Him to show them His will for their lives. Then when they are older with their backs against a wall and a decision that needs to be made, they will resist the temptation to make a decision based on their own knowledge. Instead, they will ask God to make His will and way perfectly clear.

Later that same day, they reappeared in my study. This time, they announced that they knew what God wanted them to do. I said, "All right, let's have it." Without batting an eye, they launched into telling me what they believed God wanted them to do, which was the opposite of what I knew the Lord really wanted. They said, "He told us to do (a certain thing)," and I said, "There's no way He said that. Now, go back and ask Him again, but this time, ask Him to confirm it to you in His Word." Their faces dropped because they were both old enough to know that God's Word did not contain the answer they were looking to find.

Later, as we talked about their decision, they admitted that what they wanted to do was not the best and probably not what the Lord wanted them to do. I confirmed this as I explained to them the consequences that would come from their being off track.

A Life-Changing Discovery

When we rely only on human knowledge, we end up getting into serious trouble. Always take time to ask God to show you the direction you need to take in life and expect Him to answer in one of three ways: yes, no, or wait. This is how you discover His will. We always realize that He is the One who places His dreams in our hearts. If we are drawn to a certain vocation or sense God calling us to do something that we have never dreamed possible, it could be that He is the One who is leading us and turning us in a direction that will one day glorify Him. When Jesus called Peter and John into the ministry, they were fishing on the Sea of Galilee. They had done this all their lives. However, deep inside of them was a hunger to know God. They longed for Messiah to come, and when they heard the Savior speak, something within their hearts and minds was drawn to Him. They had never experienced God's personal presence until they met the Savior. Once they did, they were ready to leave everything in order to be in the middle of His will.

He never wants us to be confined to a day-in, day-out existence. Instead, He wants us to learn to live on the higher planes of life where His blessings are and where we can glorify Him more each day. Will there be valley times? Yes, but even in the darkest valley, God lights a lantern of hope for those who believe and trust Him. He is interested in every aspect of our lives. He may not care if you wear black socks to work or gray ones, but He certainly cares how you handle the events of your day. He has a broad, overarching plan, and then He also has a desired will for you to fulfill. Along the way, we make countless decisions. In fact, each day, the decisions we make often have the ability to keep us focused and on course, or set us on a pathway that will lead us to a place of disobedience.

Let God Handle Your Life

Moses' desire to see God's people set free ended up costing him forty years in the wilderness. We can imagine that after this length of time, his goal to be "the deliverer" had started to fade. However, once this happened, he was in a position to be molded and shaped by the hand of God. Many times, we cling to our desires and dreams, not realizing that they are preventing us from experiencing God's best.

Just as the Lord had chosen Abraham, He chose Moses for a particular task. But Moses wanted to do it his way, and this was a problem. He was not ready to assume the responsibility God had planned for him until he had been broken by spending time in the desert. When we try to push ahead of God, He has no option but to place us in a position where we have to wait for Him to lead us on to the next point.

In a moment of rash behavior, Moses ended up killing an Egyptian official. Most of us would think that this would be the end of the story, but it wasn't. Many of us have failed to follow God's will and ended up sinning against Him. When people ask if sin was a part of God's plan, I realize that they have not considered the sovereignty of God. They think there is no way that sin could be a part of God's design, but they fail to realize that God is not surprised by our sin or disobedience. He knows what we must face in order to be prepared for service in His kingdom. He doesn't initiate sin, but He certainly uses it as a tool to model and shape our lives.

In Ephesians, Paul writes, "[God] chose us in Him before the foundation of the world, that we would be holy and blameless before Him. In love He predestined us to adoption [to make us His children once we trusted Him as our Savior] as sons through Jesus Christ to Himself, according to the kind intention [or good pleasure] of His will" (1:4–5). What did God choose us to do? He chose us to be holy and blameless. If sin was not a part of God's plan, then we need to ask the question, did God make a mistake and just react in the garden of Eden? Did He say, "Let's fix this quickly"? No, He knew that sin would be a part of the equation and that the problem could only be solved by faith in His Son, the Lord Jesus Christ.

God Is Our Redeemer

Moses' wrong reaction to a situation only made matters worse. God had a plan in mind, but Moses didn't read the fine print. He acted on his own intuition and authority, not God's. The day and time of Israel's deliverance was not up to Moses. It was God's to decide. However, Moses wanted to hurry things along. In righteous indignation, he acted without the Lord's direction and ended up sinning against

Him by committing murder. If you ever have wondered whether God can use you after you have bitterly failed, the lives of Moses and Abraham should settle this issue. God uses those who make their lives and hearts available to Him. His determined will for mankind is one of redemption. Part of His desired will for your life is for you to live completely devoted to Him.

While He does not want us entrapped by sin, He certainly forgives and restores. We also need to remember that He knows the plans He has for us (Jer. 29:11). You can get off track, but this does not change God's determined will. You can take a wrong turn and end up in a place in life that seems as though you are living in a very distant land. God will allow you to come to the end of yourself. More than likely, this is what He allowed to happen in Moses' life. He knew that Moses could not be used to fulfill His purpose until he had been broken by the circumstances of life. If you are going through a time of brokenness, then know that you are on your way to a great blessing. God breaks us in order to use us for a greater purpose.

God positioned Moses in a safe place—away from the temptations of an Egyptian lifestyle. From our perspective, it may have appeared that he was in isolation, but he was in God's training camp being prepared for his role as Israel's deliverer. When it was time for him to enter God's service, the Lord set a bush on fire, and Moses' heart focus was drawn to it. This is when God spoke to him. "When the LORD saw that [Moses] turned aside to look, God called to him from the midst of the bush and said, 'Moses, Moses!' And he said, 'Here I am'" (Ex. 3:4). The moment we say, "Here I am, Lord," is the moment we position ourselves to do His will.

Principles to Guide Us

There are four aspects to God's desired will:

He wants us to obey His moral laws. For example, He wants us to obey the Ten Commandments and to live according to the Sermon on the Mount (Ex. 20; Matt. 5–7). We are to love one another, forgive one another, and remain faithful to one another. The greatest commandment, however, is to love the Lord our God above everything and everyone else. When we put God first in our lives, then we will see His will unfold before us. Those who seek Him and obey Him are the people who learn to listen for His still, small voice. They watch for His ways to open up before them, and they are patient in their love for the Savior and others. There is no demanding of personal rights. Instead, there is surrender to God for He is good.

In 1 Thessalonians 5:18, Paul reminds us to be thankful, "For this is God's will for you in Christ Jesus." When we praise and thank God for His goodness toward us, the focus of our minds and hearts changes. We are no longer focused on what went wrong or our feelings of inadequacy. Instead, our hearts are set on Christ. When this happens, He is free to work in our lives in miraculous ways. Another moral law that God wants us to follow is forgiveness. Paul writes, "Do not grieve the Holy Spirit of God, by whom you were sealed for the day of redemption. Let all bitterness and wrath and anger and clamor and slander be put away from you, along with all malice. Be kind to one another, tender-hearted, forgiving each other, just as God in Christ also has forgiven you" (Eph. 4:30–32). Imagine what would happen if we truly practiced God's moral law of forgiveness. We would forgive without any thought of retribution or anger. This is exactly what God calls us to do: forgive others because He has forgiven each one of us. We do not have a legitimate right to be unforgiving toward anyone, no matter what a person has done. When we forgive someone for a wrong that has been done toward us, we are acting like Christ. It does not change the fact that the person was wrong. We are simply releasing the entire matter to God. Then we are free to live without bearing the burden of unforgiveness. At times, we may feel as though we have been crucified, but we haven't been. Jesus, however, was crucified for our sins, and He has forgiven each one of us.

He wants us to focus on the vocation He has chosen for us. God has certain intentions for your life. He wants you to discover the vocation that He created you to do. In fact, He has chosen an occupation that fits your skill, ability, talent, personality, and spiritual gift. He gave each one of these to you before you were born. He will never place you in a position that you are not equipped to handle. If He leads you into a certain career, you can be assured that He will equip you to handle it.

You may think about a certain job and decide that there is no way you can do it, but God has placed His dream within your heart. Over time, and as you pray about it, begin to imagine what it would be like to have that certain position. This is when you actually realize that God is leading, and if you will follow Him, you will experience a great blessing. God's desired will is intentional. He has a plan for the way you handle your finances, your relationships, and your vocation. However, you also have a limited free will. If you choose not to follow His guidance, then you will keep repeating the same lesson over and over again until you come to a point where you see that His will is a clear path — you have just been walking along another road.

He wants us to learn from our mistakes. One of the smartest things we can do is to pray and ask God to help us learn from our mistakes. However, many people fail to do this. They make one mistake, and instead of resting in the Lord, their minds tell them to hurry up and make another decision. They do and find that it was worse than the first one. This frustrating cycle goes on until, finally, they are exhausted and broken before the Lord. For example, one man told me that he did not believe God cared whether he was in debt or not. I said, "Oh yes, He does. God doesn't want you worrying and fretting about how you will pay the next bill. He has a plan for your life, and until you deal with your debt, you can't do it. There's a blockage, and it has to do with your finances and the way you handle the assets God has entrusted to you."

Those were the last words this man expected to hear, but what I said was true. When we are bound by anything other than the love of God, we cannot do what we were created to do for Him. Each one of us has made many mistakes. We have sinned against God and stepped out of His will at some point. The truth is that many people grew up not knowing that God had a purpose for their lives. They tried to do the best they could and ended up making one mistake after another.

The Prodigal Comes Home

How does God respond to the wrong turns we take? First, He leads us to a point where we realize we have made a horrendous mistake. When we confess our sin and foolishness to Him, He forgives us. Second, He takes the pieces of our broken lives and puts them back together. From that point on, we begin to walk through life in the light of His awesome love. When the prodigal son came home, did the father say, "You disobedient, immoral, wasteful son; you messed up your life"? No, here is what he said, "Bring me the robe of honor, a ring for my son's finger, sandals for his feet, and kill a fatted calf. We are going to have the biggest party because my son, who was lost, has come home" (Luke 15:22). Do you believe the father placed his son on the lower end of his property to live? No, he did not; once a son, always a son.

When we repent and choose to turn away from sin, God

picks up the pieces of our broken lives and puts them back together. He gives us a fresh start, new hope, and abundant encouragement. You may think your life is over because of some past sin, but it is not. There always is hope when God is involved. He is a restorer, and if you will allow Him to work, He will reshape your life so that it becomes a life of blessing, joy, and reward. When you make a decision to follow the Savior, others see His life reflected in all you do and say. They are motivated to change by your obedience.

God's greatest desire is that you would come to know Him through a personal relationship with His Son, the Lord Jesus Christ. He never wants to see you suffer because of sin. But if you do yield to temptation, He has promised to forgive (1 John 1:9). The moment you repent, you step back into His will. This does not mean that you get off the hook. The prodigal returned to his father and you can, too. I always urge those who have yielded to sin not to give up. God will take the years you have wasted and bring something good out of them. However, along the way, you may have to face the consequences of sin. This can be painful, but the Lord will be with you through the process.

He wants us to listen for His voice and to heed His warnings. For no apparent reason, God may urge you to turn left at the next traffic light. You think this is a totally ridiculous thought until you continue driving straight ahead and are hit by a car turning into the intersection. There are many times that God warns us not to do something, but we push forward thinking that we know what is best. Perhaps He cautions us not to go to a certain movie or engage in an activity that others are doing. Instead of heeding His warning, we ignore Him and usually are very sorry we did not listen to what the Spirit was saying. We can come to a point where we barely hear His voice because we have ignored Him over and over again. He may not choose to help us select the color of socks we need to wear in the morning, but He does care deeply about the many decisions you will make during the day (Ps. 139:24).

The best way to handle this is to start each morning by asking Him to guide you according to His will through the important events you will face. "Pray without ceasing" were Paul's words of instruction to the New Testament church (1 Thess. 5:17). When our hearts are attuned to His Spirit, we will follow where He leads. Abraham sensed God telling him to leave his home. He did and received God's greatest promise. As a boy, Samuel heard God call to him. He answered, knowing that he could trust the One who called to him. God has something very special for your life. He has a plan and He wants to reveal it to you, but you must be willing to listen for His voice and then to obey Him. When you do, you will discover not only His will and purpose for your life, you will experience a personal, intimate relationship with the Savior—the only Person who can lead you on to a place of eternal hope and infinite blessing.

CHAPTER NINE
The Discovery

Years ago, the ministry of In Touch was just getting started. We were still in our downtown Atlanta location and trusting God to provide new cameras for our television program. This was the first major purchase we made, and it truly was a step of faith. Even in the early years of our operation, we sensed that God was leading us to do something that was beyond our ability. This always is true when we come to a point of living in His will. He will place a goal or challenge before you, and then He will give you the desire to reach it. As our church congregation grew, so did our television audience. Every week, we received hundreds of letters telling how God was using the In Touch broadcast to change lives and motivate people to develop a personal relationship with Jesus Christ. I was encouraged and believed that we were walking right in the middle of God's will.

A Walk of Faith

However, I also realized that this would be a walk of faith. Many times, God only tells us what we need to know about His will when we need to know it. Other times, He may reveal several steps that are a part of His plan. Regardless, our duty is to respond to Him in faith. When He says step through this door, then you need to step through it. However, if you sense Him saying wait, then you would be very wise to wait and not move ahead. Moving forward without God's leading often takes us on an off-road detour. In other words, we get off track and head in a direction that is not what He has planned.

Walking in the light of God's will is a journey of faith and love. Our love for Him must become so great that we are willing to walk each day believing that wherever He leads, we will find blessing and hope and that we will also end up in a place where He will use us greatly for His kingdom work. With this in mind, we began to ask the people of our congregation to pray for God's wisdom, as we trusted Him to provide the money we needed to purchase new cameras. I was especially motivated and felt challenged to ask our members to contribute, since many had expressed a desire to see our program grow and become available to television outlets around the world. We set a Sunday aside for God's people to give toward this goal. I had no idea, however, that I would not be preaching on that day due to an illness. I was prepared to preach and certainly was looking forward to seeing what God was going to do. However, I could not get out of bed, and so I asked the Reverend Ian North to preach on that Sunday in my place.

Was it God's will that we go forward and trust Him for the money we needed? Absolutely! Did God have another plan in mind other than the one I thought was unfolding on that particular day? Evidently He did, and that is God's right—He can alter a portion of our course, and we will continue to be right in the middle of His will. He doesn't have to tell us why or give us any explanation. A major part of understanding and discovering God's will is to trust the One who is leading us. Remember, "By faith Abraham, when he was called, obeyed by going out to a place which he was to receive for an inheritance; and he went out, not knowing where he was going" (Heb. 11:8).

God Knows the Way for You to Travel

God knew exactly where he was going, but Abraham only knew that God was calling him to "go." He had enough light to see the steps he needed to take immediately in front of him, and there will be times when this is all that God gives us. What do we do? We step forward and trust Him to reveal what we need to know at the proper time in order to keep moving forward. My desire had been to preach that Sunday morning, but God had a different plan, and all I could do was to submit to that part of His will. Ian's text was from 2 Samuel 24:24. It was a sermon that only another pastor could deliver to a congregation that was standing at the crossroad of obedience. It was at that very moment that God pulled back a portion of the veil that had been covering His will for First Baptist Atlanta. None of us, at this point, knew what God knew concerning the future He had planned for this faithful congregation and the ministry of In Touch. He could see perfectly the steps that were in front of us, but we could not. This was step one in an entire staircase of steps that continues today.

Second Samuel 24 records a conversation between King David and the owner of a piece of land that David wanted to purchase as a place of sacrifice and rededication to the Lord. He had made a costly mistake by counting the fighting men in Israel's army.

So Gad came to David that day and said to him, "Go up, erect an altar to the Lord on the threshing floor of Araunah the Jebusite." David went up according to the word of Gad. Just as the Lord had commanded. Araunah looked down and saw the king and his servants crossing over toward him; and Araunah went out and bowed his face to the ground before the king. Then Araunah said, "Why has my lord the king come to his servant?" And David said, "To buy the threshing floor from you, in order to build an altar to the Lord, that the plague may be held back from the people."

Araunah said to David, "Let my lord the king take and offer up what is good in his sight. Look, the oxen for the burnt offering, the threshing sledges and the yokes of the oxen for the wood. Everything, O king, Araunah gives to the king." And Araunah said to the king, "May the LORD your God accept you." However, the king said to Araunah, "No, but I will surely buy it from you for a price, for I will not offer burnt offerings to the Lord my God which cost me nothing." So David bought the threshing floor and the oxen for fifty shekels of silver. David built there an altar to the LORD and offered burnt offerings and peace offerings. Thus the LORD was moved by prayer for the land, and the plague was held back from Israel. (2 Sam. 24:18–25)

It was human desire that tempted David to do something that was not in keeping with his life of faith before the Lord. God punished David and Israel severely for this mistake. When he realized that God had stopped the angel outside the city of Jerusalem, David rushed out to meet him.

David was a man after God's heart (Acts 13:22), not because he was talented or smart but because he loved the Lord. Deep inside of him was a desire to obey and please God. Usually, before there is a great outpouring of God's blessing through answered prayer, there is a season of repentance and personal cleansing. Ian's sermon prepared the hearts of the people for a mighty miracle—one that did not stop for months to come. As he closed the services that day, Ian asked the people in his best Australian voice, "Have you given to the Lord that which cost you something?" A silence fell over the sanctuary, and then the altar filled with people who realized God was calling them to give sacrificially to His work in the church and through His ministry of In Touch.

The following week, I was back in the pulpit preaching and wondering what God was going to do. At the close of the service, people began to come forward bringing their sacrificial offerings to the Lord. It goes without saying that

God provided the money we needed to purchase the cameras debt free. My heart was overwhelmed with gratitude to the Lord for His faithfulness and for a brief moment, I thought, *Well, that is that. We have the cameras, and now we are set.* Little did I know, but God was already at work on an even bigger set of challenges that would stretch our faith beyond anything we could imagine.

There may be seasons when you feel as though you are not really doing that much. You may even wonder if you are moving toward the goal He has given you. You are, however, and the exciting part of living within His will is that you will never grow bored. Even when you do not see His hand working, He is moving and positioning you for His purpose and to fulfill His future plan. My challenge to you is found in 2 Samuel 24:24. In order to know God's will, you have to commit yourself to Him. Have you given Him just what you feel is convenient or have you given Him something—every area of your life—that costs you in some way? The man who owned the field where David was going to offer his sacrifice to the Lord wanted to just give it to the king. However, David refused because he knew that the sacrifice he offered to God needed to be one of obedience—it had to cost him something.

A Prayer that Changes Lives

Many people try to find the will of God for their lives. They discuss it with friends, pray about it, and read countless books on the subject without discovering what God has for them. The reason many miss it is because they are too caught up in the details of life to turn their faces toward heaven with open hearts and say, "Here am I, [Lord]. Send me!" (Isa. 6:8). In his letter to the Colossian church, Paul writes his prayer for the believers in that fellowship. It was a prayer for their personal spiritual growth so they could fulfill God's will. "For this reason also, since the day we heard of it, we have not ceased to pray for you and to ask that you may be filled with the knowledge of His will in all spiritual wisdom and understanding, so that you will walk in a manner worthy of the Lord, to please Him in all respects, bearing fruit in every good work and increasing in the knowledge of God" (Col. 1:9–10).

Paul doesn't stop with the words written above. He continues because there is more for us to consider when it comes to the will of God: "Strengthened with all power, according to [God's] glorious might, for the attaining of all steadfastness and patience; joyously giving thanks to the Father, who has qualified us to share in the inheritance of the saints in Light" (vv. 11–12). When we are walking in the light of God's will, our lives will take on the characteristics that are like Him (2 Cor. 4:11, 13; Col. 2:3). We will have a sense of strength that is not derived from human ability but from a heart totally devoted to Christ. God's will involves His purpose, plan, and desire for each one of us individually. Therefore, when we come to discover His will, we can ask Him three questions:

- Lord, what is Your will for my life or this particular situation?
- How can I discover it?
- What is Your desire for me—what would please You?

There will be times when God will answer these questions, and we will know what He wants us to do in a given set of circumstances. However, many times we must spend time seeking His will and plan. We knew that God wanted the In Touch broadcast on television, but we could not conceive His greater plan for the future. Often, He only gives us the sight we need in order to do what He wants us to do next. I doubt if anyone on our staff could have handled God revealing all that was going to come our way over the next ten, twenty, or thirty years. God's plan was too awesome. We would have been overwhelmed by it, which is one of the reasons He does not reveal all that is involved in His plan. However, we can know His will for us today if we surrender our lives to Him. Those who do not do this will miss God's plan for their lives. There is no other way to put it. Either we live submitted and committed lives, or we miss the opportunity to experience His blessings and end up losing what could have been a great victory.

God's Challenge to Us

I have had people tell me, "I just don't believe in all of this." They go and do whatever they want to do and end up in a miserable state because God has told us that we were created for Him and not for ourselves (Col. 1:16). This means that He has a plan, and His desire is for us to live it out. When we get off track, life becomes very rocky and rough. The prodigal son believed he had a better plan than the one his father had for him. So he packed up his gear and walked away. This is what happened in the garden of Eden. Satan tempted Adam and Eve to question God's plan. "For God knows that in the day you eat from it your eyes will be opened, and you will be like God, knowing good and evil" (Gen. 3:5).

Eve realized there was a plan in place, but now she had to make a decision to either stick with the course that God had given them or take a different path. She chose the different path and rebelled against God by sinning and disobeying Him. What heartache she must have felt after taking a bite of the forbidden fruit! There is no way to disobey God and not realize that you have made a huge mistake. The damage was done, but God did not reject His creation. He knew their response to the enemy would lead to sin and mankind's fall. He also knows what our response will be at every turn in this life. He desires the best for us. In fact, His will and plan is one of hope and blessing (Jer. 29:11). However, we must choose to obey, and then we will receive the blessing. God's desired will for us is that we will walk according to His plan for our lives.

A Promise and a Plan

Someone reading this book may think, *I have messed up, and this is the first time I have heard any of this*. Let me remind you again that God still has a will for your life. No matter how badly you have messed up, He takes the broken pieces of your life, and through the power of His unconditional love and the blood of His Son, Jesus Christ,

He puts the pieces back together. Then He says to you, "From this point on, you are walking within My circumstantial will for your life. In light of all that is behind you, I am going to take you from where you are now to a place of blessing. As you place your trust in Me as Your Savior, I will show you how to live out the rest of your life; with My help and strength, you will live as an overcomer and not as a person who has been defeated."

The apostle Paul prayed that we would be made strong so we could fulfill God's purpose. He also prayed that we would have the spiritual wisdom we need to avoid making costly mistakes that jeopardize our walk of faith with Jesus Christ. However, when we do, God has a plan in place for our restoration so that we can begin to live in the center of His will. You don't have to flip a coin or guess what His will for your life is. You can know.

I think of the many young people who head off to college each year, hoping that they are making the right decision and career choice. When we think of God's will for our lives, we need to realize that He assumes full responsibility for telling us what it is. It is our responsibility to discover it (Matt. 7:8). No general goes to war without a battle plan, and God does not expect us to go through life without one either.

It is the nature of God to reveal His will to us. Second, it is the *promise* of God to show us what His plan is for our lives. In Psalm 32, God promises to reveal His will to us: "I will instruct you and teach you in the way which you should go; I will counsel you with My eye upon you" (v. 8). This promise is followed by a word of caution: "Do not be as the horse or as the mule which have no understanding, whose trappings include bit and bridle to hold them in check" (v. 9). This Scripture is mirrored by the words of Proverbs 3:5–7, "Trust in the LORD with all your heart and do not lean on your own understanding. In all your ways acknowledge Him, and He will make your paths straight. Do not be wise in your own eyes; fear the LORD and turn away from evil."

His Promise Leads to Spiritual Victory

God wants to make His promise and plan for your life very clear. It is part of His character to clarify what He desires for us to do. There will be times when He will map out the plan we are to follow. Other times, He will ask us to walk forward by faith, trusting Him to provide all we need when we need it. In Psalm 16, David writes, "You will make known to me the path of life; in Your presence is fullness of joy; in Your right hand there are pleasures forever"

(v. 11). I want to address a subject that I mentioned earlier, and that is the importance of the Word of God in your life. God speaks to us primarily through His Word. He also speaks to us through the presence of the Holy Spirit and words spoken by a godly friend or pastor. At no time will the counsel of the Spirit go against what is written in God's Word, and neither should the counsel we receive from others. What we hear and read always should line up with God's Word. This is because His Word is our life's compass. In it, we find direction for the decisions we need to make today and in the future.

If you want to find God's will for your life, you have to begin by reading and studying His Word. This is where He will begin to reveal His plan, and it is where we start to understand the nature of God. You can't know Him apart from His Word. Yet many people try to do this very thing. They go to church on Sundays hoping they will find an answer to their problems. They turn on the television praying that someone will provide a solution to their situation. Many preachers today will tell their audiences that they can experience a "breakthrough" in what they are facing, but apart from the Word of God, this is impossible. The way we come to know God is by reading the Bible. How we learn to live life within the framework of His will is by studying and applying the principles given to us within Scripture. Once a person understands this truth, he or she can know God's will for most situations.

In 1 Samuel 23:2, David learned to seek God's wisdom before heading off to battle. A group of men came to him saying, "'Behold, the Philistines are fighting against Keilah and are plundering the threshing floors.' So David inquired of the LORD, saying, 'Shall I go and attack these Philistines?' And the LORD said to David, 'Go and attack the Philistines and deliver Keilah.'" God gave him the wisdom he needed, but he had to ask the Lord for guidance, and we do too.

A New Way of Living

He may not tell you whether to wear brown or black shoes tomorrow, but you can know whether He wants you to move forward or stay where you are. His Word will help you to learn how He thinks; and once you begin to understand this, you will be able to begin to know His plan for your life. It is not just the study of God's Word that will help you in your discovery of His plan for your life; it is the understanding that once you accept Christ as your Savior, you become a new person. Life changes dramatically. You are no longer operating under the old system. A new one is in operation. Paul writes in 2 Corinthians, "Therefore if anyone is in Christ, he is a new creature; the old things passed away; behold, new things have come" (5:17).

God also reveals His will to us through circumstances. Even though he was in prison, Paul wrote to the Philippian church saying, "I want you to know, brethren, that my circumstances have turned out for the greater progress of the gospel, so that my imprisonment in the cause of Christ has become well known throughout the whole praetorian guard and to everyone else" (Phil. 1:12–13). Even though Paul's circumstances did not look good, God used them to accomplish His will. We must be willing to go the extra mile with God. Just as we said earlier when talking about Abraham, God instructed him to move forward, and he obeyed based on the fact that the One who was speaking to him was a sovereign God. Your circumstances may be very trying, and you do not understand how God will ever gain glory from what you are facing. He will, and if you set the focus of your heart on knowing and pleasing Him, not only will you experience His blessings, but those around you will be blessed as well. Jesus has promised never to leave you. This means every single moment of your life, He is living within you (John 15:4, 7).

CHAPTER TEN

The Adventure Begins

The weather report was shocking. For the fourth time in a year, a hurricane was heading for the Gulf of Mexico and for Florida. Despite the prayers of millions of Christians, this storm, like the ones before it, seemed determined to bring destruction to a massive area of land that had not recovered from the earlier storms. There was a state of panic as people either evacuated or remained glued to their television screens watching news and weather reports.

Somewhere in the hurricane's path was a Christian retirement community that also housed an assisted living and nursing home facility. As news media broadcasted live reports concerning the storm's path and the people at the national weather station tracked its every move, the residents of this small Florida community did what they had practiced many times; they calmly walked to their designated storm shelter—a parking garage that had been outfitted with removable storm siding—and settled in for what promised to be a very long night. They had been instructed to bring lounge chairs, water, and snacks.

Faith in an All-Powerful God

As the evening approached, residents became aware that they could receive a direct hit from the hurricane. However, instead of striking fear in their hearts, the howling wind and the turbulent rains only created what one resident called "a cozy environment." Finally, someone began to sing an old hymn, and soon others joined. Words of prayer and praise also filled the dusty parking deck, and it became a shelter of peace for God's people in a time of horrendous trial.

Hours later, the danger had passed and residents were allowed to return to their homes. Many joined hands and formed a human chain as they walked back to their homes and to their rooms. Suddenly a glorious sunset broke through the clouds, and the residents looked up to see the sky streaked with color. Even in this time of trial, it was as if the peace of God hovered over them.

How many of us would dare to look at our broken circumstances and storm-driven lives and see the color of a sunset or a sunrise? God does every time, and He tells us:

I know the plans I have for you. (Jer. 29:11)

I have inscribed your name on the palms of My hand.
(Isa. 49:16)

Nothing can separate you from My love. (Rom. 8:35)

My love casts out fear. (1 John 4:18)

I will never leave you. (John 14:18)

My thoughts of you are too numerous to count.
(Ps. 40:5)

I go to prepare a place for you and you will be with Me.
(John 14:2)

We are never outside of God's overarching plan. It may seem that we have taken a wrong turn, gotten off track, or that the sorrows of this life have caught up with us; but God is never surprised by our circumstances, and He is never out of control. There are no storms too great and no problems too deep for Him to solve. No matter what you may face, when you surrender your life and your situation to Him, God will place a sense of peace deep within your heart, and you will come to know Him in a more intimate way.

His Plan Never Changes

The situations of life may change, but God never does (Heb. 13:8). He does not alter His determined plan for our lives. We can step away from it, but He still has a determined will that is at work molding and shaping us and leading us back to Him. Many people make mistakes and worry that they have disappointed God, but we cannot disappoint an all-knowing God. He knew how we would respond even before temptation pulled at our hearts. He is committed to loving us through the sorrow of our sin and helping us get back on track. Someone reading these words cannot believe life can be lived without the influence of drugs or alcohol, but it can. Others wonder how God can possibly have a plan for their lives now that their spouse has left them, but He does. He is not distracted or changed by our circumstances. He is our Deliverer, and His truth will set us free from the bondage of sin, doubt, fear, worry, and anxiety. It heals our wounded hearts and opens up our lives to the possibility of being used once again, or maybe for the first time, for God's glory.

Paul writes to the believers living in the city of Colossae, "For this reason also, since the day we heard of it, we have not ceased to pray for you and to ask that you may be filled with the knowledge of His will in all spiritual wisdom and understanding" (Col. 1:9). Once we realize that God has a promise for our lives, we begin to understand that this promise involves every area of life. It doesn't matter whether we are young or old; God's plan begins before we take our first breath and does not end until we are standing in His presence. "God causes all things to work together for good to those who love [Him], to those who are called according to His purpose" (Rom. 8:28). This is God's promised will to every man and woman who comes to know Him as Savior and Lord. No one is excluded from His plan or purpose. However, we are the ones who must take hold of this promise and choose to live our lives for Him.

Peter could have remained on shore the day that Jesus asked to use his fishing boat. He could have said, "No way! I am not going to launch my boat and go back out on the sea. I just got back from being out there, and, to be honest, there are no fish. Today is not a good day to go fishing." However, we know that Peter did not say any of this. He looked into the eyes of Jesus and saw something much deeper than he had ever seen. Within the eyes of Christ was all that he had prayed to know and discover. Though he did not know how to express it, Peter knew a new world of hope and possibility awaited him, and the first step to experiencing this was summed up in his words of obedience, "Master, . . . I will do as you say and let down the nets" (Luke 5:5).

A few minutes later, Peter's nets began to fill with fish. The catch was so great that they began to break, and he called to his friends to come and help him. They responded by sailing their boats to the same spot. However, these boats also filled up and began to sink. Peter "fell down at Jesus' feet, saying, 'Go away from me Lord, for I am a sinful man!'" (Luke 5:8). None of this was a result of luck or coincidence. There is no such thing in the life of a believer. This was a planned event—a moment in Peter's life that fit perfectly with the will of God.

An Exciting Adventure Begins

Bending over to touch the shoulder of His new disciple, Jesus said, "Do not fear, from now on you will be catching men" (Luke 5:10). When Peter and the others reached the shore, they left everything and followed Christ. Their greatest desire had come true. They had found the Savior, and they were right on course to begin an amazing journey that would last for eternity. God wants you to know that He has a wondrous promise for your life. It is a promise that involves His perfect plan and one that will bring joy, hope, and countless opportunities. Will you raise your sails, head out into deep water, and allow the winds of His purpose and victory to blow through your life so others will come to know the Savior's love too?

Have You Accepted God's Greatest Gift?

Our heavenly Father has prepared many special gifts and blessings for His children. However, the greatest gift is the gift of eternal life that He gives to those who come to Him through faith in His Son, Jesus. If you have never invited Him to be your Savior and Lord, you can right now by praying this simple prayer:

Father, I know that I am a sinner. I believe Jesus died on the cross for my sins and paid my sin debt in full, cleansing me of my past failures and guilt. I surrender control of my life to You today. Make me the person You have designed me to be. I pray this in Jesus' name. Amen.

If you sincerely prayed this prayer to God, then according to God's Word, you have been born again (1 Peter 1:3)!

I want to challenge you to take positive steps to grow in your new faith. Please take time to visit www.charlesstanley.com, and become involved in our study program. Also, be sure to tell someone of your decision to follow Jesus, and find a church that will teach the uncompromised truth of God's Word. Today is the first day of a journey that will someday lead you into the presence of your heavenly Father, who has loved you since the beginning of time.

HOW TO LET GOD
SOLVE YOUR
PROBLEMS

My soul finds rest in God alone;
my salvation comes from him.
He alone is my rock and my salvation;
he is my fortress, I will never be shaken.
Psalm 62:1–2 NIV

CONTENTS

INTRODUCTION

Can Good Come Out
of This Situation?

In times of great difficulty, people often wonder how they will be able to continue. The pain may seem too great for them to handle or the sorrow too deep. They often ask, "Will anything good come out of this tragedy?" When God is involved, the answer is always yes!

However, it may take time—in some cases, years—before you realize God's providential hand is always at work in your life. When you do, you also will come to know that you were never alone, forgotten, or abandoned. At every turn, Jesus was beside you.

David writes, "Even though I walk through the valley of the shadow of death, I fear no evil, for You are with me" (Ps. 23:4). There is only one way to face adversity, and that is by faith in Jesus Christ. Either you can struggle against life's difficulties, or you can turn them over to the Lord and ask Him to give you the wisdom and strength you need to handle each one. When you commit your life to Him, He will take care of all that concerns you. That is His promise. David writes,

"The LORD will accomplish what concerns me; Your lovingkindness, O LORD, is everlasting; do not forsake the works of Your hands" (Ps. 138:8).

In Philippians, the apostle Paul reminds us that there is no limitation to the accomplishments we can achieve if our hearts are set on Christ. He writes, "I can do all things through Him who strengthens me" (4:13). With these words, Paul reveals the secret to dealing with life's hard-to-handle challenges. It is dependency—dependency on a sovereign, omnipotent God, who loves us with an everlasting love. Over his lifetime, the problems and trials Paul faced were anything but light. In fact, he tells us in 2 Corinthians,

> Five times I received from the Jews thirty-nine lashes. [Forty lashes was a sentence of sure death.] Three times I was beaten with rods, once I was stoned, three times I was shipwrecked, a night and a day I have spent in the deep.
>
> I have been on frequent journeys, in dangers from rivers, dangers from robbers, dangers from my countrymen, dangers from the Gentiles, dangers in the city, dangers in the wilderness, dangers on the sea, dangers among false brethren; I have been in labor and hardship, through many sleepless nights, in hunger and thirst, often without food, in cold and exposure. Apart from such external things, there is the daily pressure on me of concern for all the churches. Who is weak without my being weak? Who is led into sin without my intense concern? If I have to boast, I will boast of what pertains to my weak-

ness. The God and Father of the Lord Jesus, He who is blessed forever, knows that I am not lying. (11:24–31)

From a human perspective, Paul should have been dead, but he was alive to do the will of God. He writes, "For even when we came into Macedonia our flesh had no rest, but we were afflicted on every side: conflicts without, fears within. But God, who comforts the depressed, comforted us" (2 Cor. 7:5–6). When you face sorrow, heartbreak, and disappointment of any kind, He will do the same for you. He will comfort you so that you will not grow weary (Isa. 40:31). He will teach you how to trust Him to a greater degree, and He also will show you how to comfort others who are hurting and facing tremendous trials (2 Cor. 1:4–7). The problem that you are struggling with today may be one that has lingered for a long time—so long, in fact, you may wonder if it will ever be resolved and if life will return to being normal. But adversity, like nothing else, has the ability to bring about solid, constructive change in your life. When you allow God to bear your burdens, this change will result in a closer fellowship with Him.

As you read through this book, I want to challenge you to alter the way you view life's problems and trials. Instead of cowering in fear when difficulties come, step out in faith and trust God to deal with your circumstances. Without a doubt, He will teach you to face life's problems the way Joseph, Elijah, Moses, Paul, and Peter did—by staying the course, fighting the good fight of faith, and developing a new attitude toward the problems of life. In fact, when it comes to adversity, God always has a greater plan in mind.

It is my prayer that you will come to know the love of the Savior in a much deeper way. Then when life does become dark and stormy, you will immediately know to turn to God in prayer, trusting Him to care for you. You will watch in amazement as He works on your behalf. Therefore, believe, pray, and know that if adversity touches your life, God is at work, and He will bring you through this season of difficulty victoriously!

CHAPTER 1

No Problem Too Great

Nothing was gentle or kind about Hurricane Katrina. What began as a small tropical storm on August 24, 2005, quickly became a category one hurricane as it passed just north of Key West, Florida. At the time, no one would have thought that in less than four days, this storm would turn into a raging category five hurricane with wind speeds surpassing 170 mph, but this is exactly what it did.

After frightening residents of Key West and chasing tourists away from the southernmost point of the United States, the storm turned northward and headed out into the Gulf of Mexico where warmer-than-normal water temperatures fueled its growing fury. Two days later, weather forecasters were stunned by the satellite images they were receiving detailing the storm's track. At one point the hurricane, along with its outer rain bands, completely filled the Gulf of Mexico. Even more frightening was the fact that the hurricane had trained its eye on the coastal areas of Louisiana, Mississippi, and the western third of Alabama.

Residents began frantically packing cars and seeking any route of escape. Highways quickly became slow-moving parking lots as people fled from the inevitable. Countless others, however, believed they could outlast the storm on their own. Some said they had no way to leave the area. They boarded up their houses or sought refuge in shelters, but to little avail. As Katrina approached land, local government officials realized this storm would be physically, emotionally, and mentally devastating to everyone in its path. Destruction would be mammoth, and recovery would not be easy or quick.

Just as it made landfall, Hurricane Katrina weakened to a category four. But its sustained winds hovered at 145 mph, and Americans witnessed one of the most deadly storms in history plow ashore. Close to 1,300 people died in storm-related deaths, and damage estimates are reported to be more than $200 billion. More than a million people were displaced from their homes. Countless individuals were separated from loved ones. At the time, the one question on everyone's mind seemed to be: How could this have happened?

Winds of Adversity

The winds of adversity blow strong. They also blow in every direction. They do not discriminate between rich or poor, weak or strong. Though many people try desperately to avoid difficulty and hardship, sooner or later adversity will strike our lives. This is because no one is exempt from sorrow, heartache, disappointment, and even sudden tragedy. When the storm does hit, it can cause a multitude of problems: fear, anxiety, and anger. It can tempt us to doubt God's goodness and to feel as though the very foundation of our lives will crumble beneath us.

In the aftermath of a storm—whether emotional or physical—we may be tempted to wonder if we will ever be able to put the pieces of our lives back together. After all, how do we recover from the heartfelt loss of our homes, the death of a friend or a spouse, or the sharp and painful feelings that come as a result of divorce? How can we go on after hearing the news that we have been let go from a job we loved? Will we ever get past the stinging reality of finding out that the husband or wife who once vowed to love until "death do us part" loves someone else? Is there any cure for the loneliness, isolation, and depression we are feeling? Will life ever return to a normal pace after suffering a long and serious illness? The answer to these questions is found through faith in God. In the aftermath of any storm, He is the only One we can turn to for encouragement.

Many times, people search through the debris of their lives looking for signs of hope and anything still connected to the life they once knew. Even if everything we regarded as familiar changes, God remains the same (Heb. 13:8). He is our eternal anchor in stormy and difficult times (Heb. 6:19).

And He has promised never to forsake those who love Him (Deut. 31:6, 8; Heb. 13:5).

You may be thinking, *My life has been shattered by tragedy, and I just don't believe there is any hope available for me. In fact, I got up this morning, went to my office, and a few minutes into my day, my manager told me the company no longer needed me. I have been fired, and now I feel numb and wonder what I will do to take care of my family's needs.* God is never surprised by the difficulties you face. He knows all about the circumstances of your life before they unfold. Some come as a result of living in a fallen world. Others are the result of sin, but even when you have turned away from Him, there is hope.

There are also seasons to life—times when the winds of adversity hit without warning and with the force of a category five hurricane. And if a person lives long enough, he or she will experience some type of adversity. Being prepared for seasons of difficulty gives you the motivation you need to stay the course when trouble comes. You also can learn how to examine a problem rationally and to turn it over to the Lord rather than succumb to feelings of depression, guilt, or shame.

More than likely, you know what it feels like to stare sorrow and disappointment in the face. For the person who has picked up this book with the hope of finding an answer to the heaviness he or she is feeling, there is great news: God has given us His promise of restoration. He tells us in Joel 2:25, "I will make up to you for the years that the swarming locust has eaten, the creeping locust, the stripping locust and the gnawing locust." In this passage, the Lord was speaking of the nation of Israel. However, there is an eternal principle involved that we can apply to our lives. When you trust God with your circumstances, He not only will help you solve whatever problem you are facing, but He will restore all that has been lost in the process. The restoration may come in a different way. Nevertheless, it will come, and you will be able to sense God's goodness in the process.

He knows when we face difficulties that are beyond our ability to handle, and He promises hope and restoration when our faith is in Him alone. In Deuteronomy 30:1–3, He says, "So it shall be when all of these things have come upon you, the blessing and the curse which I have set before you, and you call them to mind . . . and you return to the LORD your God and obey Him with all your heart and soul . . . then the LORD your God will restore you." The Lord is the One who provides the strength and courage we need to go forward by faith, trusting Him with our future even when the sun does not appear for many days and months. He is not the author of evil, nor did His original design include devastation and heartache. However, He uses both of these for His purpose and glory, and for our blessing. And it is in times of extreme difficulty that He develops our character and strengthens us spiritually, while helping us to grow deeper in our faith in Him.

Adversity comes as a result of two different aspects. It

often strikes as a result of living in a fallen environment. While God originally created this world to be perfect, Adam and Eve sinned, and we are now living with the consequences of their disobedience. We also experience adversity when we fail to obey God. All sin has consequences—some much more serious than others. While the consequences of sin are very serious, God never stops loving us, and when we acknowledge our need of Him and that we have made a wrong turn, He is quick to restore our fellowship with Him.

God Specializes in Hope

You may think that in your disobedience, you have gone too far. Nothing is beyond His reach—no sin is too great for Him to handle. He is God, and He is sovereign. He loves you with an infinite love, and there may be times when He will allow adversity to strike so that you will turn back to Him. In their agony, Adam and Eve cried out, and the Lord moved on their behalf. Though He cast them out of the garden of Eden, He made garments for them to wear (Gen. 3:21). He also set into motion His plan of redemption for you and me, which included the coming of His Son, the Savior of the world. The Bible tells us, "For God so loved the world [you], that He gave His only begotten Son, that whoever believes in Him shall not perish, but have eternal life" (John 3:16).

God is greater than any form of evil. He is alive and present with us through the power of His Holy Spirit in the lives of those who have accepted Jesus Christ as Savior and Lord. This means that not only do we have a sure hope for what seems to be the most hopeless of circumstances, but we also have a loving Savior who comforts us in our times of trial and heartache (2 Cor. 1:3–4). He has a plan for your life, even if it has been damaged and torn apart by the winds of adversity (Jer. 29:11). You may think that there is no way He could ever love you, but He does. He created you in love for the purpose of knowing and loving you. Catastrophic events that involve innocent people are not the result of anything we have done wrong. God is not a stern judge who is sitting up in heaven waiting for the right moment to crush us for our actions.

He is a God of love, but when we make unwise decisions, He allows us to face the consequences of these wrong choices. Adam disobeyed God and therefore suffered for failing to do what God had commanded him to do. When we violate a principle of God, we can expect to suffer some type of adversity. Many times, we are quick to recognize what we have done and take the right steps to correct the situation. Other times, we may not be as quick to respond correctly, and the adversity intensifies until we respond to God's correction.

There are consequences to sin—actions we are sure will not hurt anyone. Words thoughtlessly spoken bring deep hurt to a person's life and can have a lasting impact. We may casually dismiss our actions as being said or done in fun, but God thinks differently and will prick our consciences until we acknowledge that what we have done is wrong. A few years ago, I sat in my office listening to a young man who had come by the church to drop off a few things and asked to see me. After a few minutes of light conversation, I became aware that storm clouds were not only building in this man's life, but they were about to break open.

When we think about stormy situations, we usually believe these include an unexpected sickness, an unforeseen financial distress, or an unpreventable accident. This is true, but many of the storms we face also come as the result of personal sin—sin that could have been prevented by just saying no to a single thought of temptation. This was the case in this man's life, and he had a lot of work to do before he could experience the unconditional trust of his family again. However, he was able to make it because he sought forgiveness and refuge in Christ. With God's help, he was able to turn away from the sin that almost destroyed his family.

What type of storm are you facing today? Do you realize that even if it has appeared as a result of something you have done, God is in it with you? You are never alone. He will not forsake you when you call to Him and admit that you failed to follow His principles and need His forgiveness and wisdom to right what has been done wrong. He is your unshakable refuge, and though you may have strayed, He will restore you when you turn your heart back to Him.

How do you handle adversity? What do you do when the walls of your life collapse and there seems to be no point of retreat for you? How do you go on to face the next day and the day after that? In the back of the lonely, dark cave of Adullam, we can imagine David's tears running heavy down his face. He had never been in a place like this one. Sure, he had been on the battlefield facing fierce soldiers of war, but he had never been here, and certainly never alone. Alone! That is the way he felt. Though four hundred men were with him, more than likely he felt alone, and the pain he experienced was horrifying (1 Sam. 22:1). How did this happen? Wasn't he the anointed king of Israel? Didn't he have a secure place to live, a home in Jerusalem, and friends who opened their lives to him? There was nothing in this place to welcome him except a handful of sandy soil and the constant dripping of seeping water emerging from the rocky walls that concealed him from his enemy, King Saul.

When David bowed for Samuel to anoint him king, he had no idea his life was headed for turmoil and trouble. In fact, more than likely, he imagined triumph and victory. Instead, he found himself writing these few words of a prayer and psalm to God: "Be gracious to me, O God, be gracious to me, for my soul takes refuge in You; and in the shadow of Your wings I will take refuge until destruction passes by. I will cry to God Most High, to God who accomplishes all things for me. He will send from heaven and save me" (Ps. 57:1–3).

No matter how painful your situation may be, God has a greater purpose in mind for the heartache that you are suffering. Over the weeks, months, and even years that followed, those few moments spent in a cave of discouragement were never forgotten by David. He had learned a simple principle—one that would rule his life: trust God with your circumstances, and leave all the consequences to Him. He was molding David's life for a greater challenge and a greater blessing. He had a plan in mind for the disappointments His servant faced, just as He does for us. Perhaps the winds of adversity are blowing hard against your life, and you cannot begin to think how you will make it through another day, let alone another week. You tell your friends that you feel numb and defeated. God, however, wants you to lift your head so you can see the many promises, opportunities, and blessings He has waiting for you.

The Wrong View

There is a popular religious view in our world today that is totally opposite of what the Bible teaches. It tells us that if we will trust God, believe in Him, and make sure our faith is focused in the right direction, we will never have to face adversity. Nothing could be farther from the truth. The fact is that during our lifetimes, each one of us will face many trials. Some will be simple to weather, while others will be much more difficult. Having the wrong view of adversity can lead to serious problems. This can cause us to doubt God when we need to buckle down and trust Him to an even greater degree. It also can tempt us to become cynical and bitter, especially when we adopt a "poor me" attitude.

When you face adversity, ask God to help you understand His will and purpose for the difficulty. He may not tell you all you want to know. But over time, you will find that He gives you exactly what you need at the right time. One of the surest ways to experience God's hope is to read His Word. God's unconditional love and restoration are woven throughout the Bible. It chronicles the amazing, unconditional love of a holy and righteous God who loves you with an everlasting love. Within its pages, you will discover that you are not alone. Each one of the saints of God faced times of tremendous trial and discouragement. They struggled with feelings of fear and thoughts of defeat. But they were relentless in their faith because they were convinced that the One who promised to deliver them from heartache and sorrow would do it, and He did. The awesome truth is that He is willing to do the same for you today.

CHAPTER 2

The Test of Endurance

I have been a Christian many years, and as I think about my life, I realize God has allowed one storm after another to blow through my life—one heartache, trial, burden, or tribulation after another. Each time, He has spoken to my heart, but I have never heard Him say, "Don't worry about a thing. Just relax."

Instead, He often says simply, "Trust Me." There is something about hearing these two words that brings a sense of peace to my heart. I may feel troubled over a decision and wonder what will happen next. However, when I sense God saying, "Trust Me," I stop thinking about all that could or could not happen and begin to rest in His presence and care. I also find that when I let go of my need to work something out, He handles all the details of my circumstances perfectly. Later in his life, David faced a very difficult set of circumstances. His life was being threatened again. Yet we find that he placed his hope in God and not in his own ability as king. In Psalm 55:22, we discover the key to his confidence. He writes, "Cast your burden upon the LORD and He will sustain you; He will never allow the righteous to be shaken." The word *cast* literally means to "roll over on God." In other words, David is telling us to roll the burdens of our hearts onto the Lord. After all, He is the only One who has the power, the insight, and the ability to handle each one.

The apostle Peter echoes David's words. He writes: "Cast all your anxiety on him [Christ] because he cares for you" (1 Pet. 5:7 NIV). Only here, he tells us to roll our feelings of anxiety, fear, and discouragement over onto Christ our Savior, knowing He will lift us up and give us the guidance we need to face every threat. Therefore, when all hope seems to be gone and when sorrow or sin has clouded your way, ask God to reveal Himself to you, and tell Him that you want His will for your life and that you are asking Him to forgive you if you have knowingly disobeyed Him.

A Test of Endurance

I have no idea what problem you are facing, but I know you are not alone. You may look at your life and wonder, "God, how did I get in this mess?" "Why did You allow me to fall to this place?" "How will I ever get out of this?" "When I look at my life, the only thing I can see is a long, dark tunnel, and there is not even a ray of light falling down. Is there any hope for me?" As far as you may be concerned, the walls of life have closed in on you, and there is no place to turn. Each of us will walk through times of darkness when all we will want to do is find a cave and crawl into it, but we must not do this. All of us have wept over the heartaches, struggles, trials, and temptations that we have had to face. We did not know how we would find our way through the darkness. I know there have been times in my own life when I have gone to bed at night wondering, "Lord, what are You going to do about all of this?" I also have prayed, "God, why don't You do something?" One of the most wonderful aspects of our Lord's life is the fact that He cried out on the cross, "My God, My God, why have You forsaken Me?" (Mark 15:34).

If we were honest, we would admit that there have been times when we have wanted to cry out, "Lord, why are You forsaking me? Why don't You do something in my life?" He knows when you walk through the valley of temptation—when you want to do what is right, but you just do not seem to be able to do it. You try, but you fail, and then you want to quit, to give up and walk away. But you do not have to give up. Do not ever consider giving up. There is something about giving up that carries an awesome penalty and sense of disappointment.

The *first* thing I want you to understand is this: when we give up, we run the risk of damaging our self-esteem. Something also happens to our attitudes. Instead of life just looking dark for a season, problems suddenly seem insurmountable. We lose sight of the truth that nothing is too difficult for God. Abraham and Sarah thought there was no way that they would ever have children. Both were far too old. However, God reminded them of His promise and then said, "Is anything too difficult for the LORD? At the appointed time I will return to you, at this time next year, and Sarah will have a son" (Gen. 18:14). This is exactly what happened! The storms of life are not confined to physical storms. They can be emotional and mental. They also can come as the result of a sincere disappointment. However, when we seek Him, God gives us the ability to do what Moses did: "He endured, as seeing Him who is unseen" (Heb. 11:27).

The *second* thing that happens when we give up is that we miss out on the tremendous blessing God has for us, especially for those who are willing to undergo and endure hardship and difficulty. The Israelites had been given the promised land, but they did not go in and claim it. Securing the land seemed too hard, and they became overwhelmed by the prospect of doing what they knew God had given them to do. Instead of obeying the Lord from the beginning, they sent twelve spies to see if the land was good. Sure enough, ten of the men brought back a negative report saying that there were giants in the land and more than likely, everyone would die (Num. 13:27–31). Two men, Joshua and Caleb, had an opposite view. They believed the land was indeed good and that with God's help they could take it from their enemies.

Sadly, negativism won out, and the people refused to enter the land. God was angry at the nation of Israel. In fact, an entire generation passed away before Israel had another opportunity to go into the land that God had given them. Only Joshua, Caleb, and Moses survived. The next time they surveyed the land, they came back and said, "Surely the LORD has given all the land into our hands; moreover, all the inhabitants of the land have melted away before us" (Josh. 2:24). The first time around, Israel had missed the blessing of God, but the second time, they had learned the lesson of obedience and entered into God's promised blessing.

The *third* thing that happens when we give up is that we limit God's use of our lives. There will be times when the battle you face seems to be too much for you. In fact, you cannot imagine how you will make it through, but God does. He knows exactly what you need and when you need it. If you give up now, there is no telling what you will miss. God has a purpose for the pain you are suffering. He used adversity in Job's life to refine his servant and prepare him for an even greater blessing than he once had. With God's strength, Job withstood the enemy's wicked blows, and the Lord was glorified, though Job suffered a great loss. Are you ready to step over into the promised blessing that God has prepared for you? Or have you been tempted to turn around and run at the thought of having to endure for a long period of time?

Before her retirement, Supreme Court Justice Sandra Day O'Connor was asked what her confirmation hearings had been like. She looked straight into the eyes of the interviewer and said, "A test of endurance." We gain nothing in this life apart from endurance, which involves two things—patience and time. Endurance means that I am willing to stay at my post— where God has placed me—until He tells me to move forward. It also means that no matter how hard life may become, I will follow wherever He leads. I will remain committed to waiting on Him for His direction and guidance. In 2 Timothy 2:3, Paul tells us to be willing to "suffer hardship . . . as a good soldier of Christ Jesus." This is why it is critical to have a right focus. If we are worried and fretting over what will happen tomorrow, we will not be able to make godly decisions today. In fact, we will not even be able to hear God's voice because we will be so caught up in the chatter of our doubts and fears. This is what happened to the nation of Israel. They listened to the enemy's lies—telling them that they could not go into the land and claim what God had given to them.

If God has called you to a certain task, you can be sure that He will equip you to do it. Trust Him, and when He says, "Step forward," take your first step and you will see His blessing open up before you. You may have to face affliction and persecution. However, when you do, God will give you the strength and ability you need to do this without complaining. Instead of becoming frustrated to the point of giving up, you will be able to face the difficulty with a sure confidence, knowing that the same God who has allowed these circumstances to touch your life has promised to bear the burden for you and walk beside you every step of the way. He is your burden-bearer. You do not have to carry the weight of sorrow by yourself because He will carry it for you.

Jesus told His followers in Matthew 11:28–30, "Come to Me, all who are weary and heavy-laden, and I will give you rest. Take My yoke upon you and learn from Me, for I am gentle and humble in heart, and you will find rest for your souls. For My yoke is easy and My burden is light." We are the ones who make sorrow and heartache even more difficult to bear. Many times, we believe Satan's lies. Problems arise, and we immediately think that life is over or that we will never rebound from our problems. Nothing, however, is impossible with God (Matt. 19:26).

Five Principles That Lead to Victory

There are five principles that will help you turn away from the temptation to give up. They also will help you understand how to trust God even when it seems that there is no end in sight to the trouble you are experiencing.

Stop focusing on your circumstances and begin focusing on the promises of God.
The night that Jesus walked across a stormy sea to the boat carrying His disciples, Peter shouted out to the Lord, "Lord, if it is You, command me to come to You on the water" (Matt. 14:28). Jesus told him to "come," and Peter got out of the boat and began to walk to Christ. However, halfway there, he began to notice the strength of the wind and the height of the waves, and before he knew it, he was sinking and crying out to Christ for help. Jesus reached down and saved him. Then He said, "You of little faith, why did you doubt?" (v. 31). We can almost hear Jesus' words to His disappointed disciple, "You were doing so well. Why did you stop? You would have made it, but you took your eyes off of Me and began to worry

about the storm that was around you. Do you not know that I am your peace in time of difficulty and trouble?"

When he was fifty-five years old, J. C. Penney was tempted to think that his life was over. He was in terrible health, along with being seven million dollars in debt. He could have said, "I give up. I quit. I declare bankruptcy." However, he refused to focus on his circumstances. Instead, he majored on the possibilities, and by the time he was ninety years old, he had not only regained what he had lost, but he was the head of a tremendous financial empire—one that continues to bear his name today. You may feel as though you just want to give up, but giving up is easy. Anyone can quit and walk away from life. However, it takes courage to go on when it appears that every avenue has been blocked and every opportunity removed. The pathway to hope and victory often runs straight through the valley of adversity—one that is difficult and full of heartache, affliction, and suffering. The key to endurance is not found in running to this friend and then another for advice. It is found only at the feet of Jesus, where we also learn to say no to discouragement and yes to God. After all, He is the One who knows you by name and has a marvelous plan for your life.

Be willing to make a commitment not to give up.
Only Jesus Christ suffered more than Job did. Job was God's man, and Satan knew it. He also was sure that Job would fail the test. This is why he requested an opportunity to test Job's faithfulness. God allowed it, and in the heat of the adversity, when it appeared that his misery could not become worse,

Job declared his faith in God: "Though He slay me, I will hope in Him" (Job 13:15).

After Christ's death, the disciples were full of fear and discouragement. In fact, even after they had seen the Lord, they continued to wonder what they would do. Finally, they returned to their old jobs as fishermen. When Jesus found them one morning, they were on the Sea of Galilee throwing nets out into the water (John 21). Weeks earlier, they were His disciples, following Him throughout the countryside, listening to Him teach, and being trained to minister His truth to others. Then the dream appeared to fall apart. The goal became unreachable, and they wanted to give up. But Jesus came to them, and He comes to each one of us who is experiencing feelings of rejection, loneliness, defeat, sorrow, and depression. He does not forget those who love Him.

Once the disciples realized that nothing had ended and their greatest fears were unfounded, they made a commitment to the Lord and never drifted off course again. Every one of them, except for John, died a martyr's death. John was imprisoned on the Isle of Patmos where he wrote the book of Revelation. When things become difficult, we are tempted to think, *I don't have to put up with this anymore. God doesn't expect me to have to face this.* Many times He does. He allows trials to come our way so that we will turn to Him and learn how to live this life in total dependence on Him.

Claim your position in Christ.

First Peter tells us that He loves us regardless of our circumstances (5:7). The author of Hebrews 13:5 reminds us that no matter what we are going through—whatever circumstances we are facing, a sovereign loving God says, "I have wrapped My arms around you, and I am going to see you through this. I'm not going to desert you anywhere along the way." "When the attorney comes with the papers for you to sign, I will be with you." "When your children walk out and you find out they have been using drugs, I will be there to encourage you and give you the strength to hold on." He will never leave us and never forsake us (Heb. 13:5). You can cast your cares on Him, and He will protect and care for you forever.

Cling to the anchor of your soul—the Lord Jesus Christ.
The enemy may try to unleash an avalanche of doubt and fear, but when you are clinging to the One who loves you with an everlasting love, you will be safe and secure. There will be no reason to doubt or to stop moving forward. No matter what anyone says to you, once you know that God has set the course for you to travel, be willing to cling and endure, and you will enjoy His goodness in a way that you have never felt. When you are anchored to Christ, you will not be blown off course.

Cry out to God.
In Psalm 34, David writes, "This poor man cried, and the LORD heard him and saved him out of all his troubles. The angel of the LORD encamps around those who fear Him, and rescues them" (vv. 6–7). Peter cried out to Jesus, and the Lord responded immediately. He put out His hand and pulled the brash and bold disciple up and out of the surf. There have been many times in my life when I did not know what to do. The only

thing I had to stand upon was the Word of God. There seemed to be no solution to my problem. I have gone to bed and cried myself to sleep calling out for God to help me. Each time, God has answered my prayer. There has never been a time when He failed to help me. When I cried out in desperation and futility and in absolute dependency on Him, He responded to my plea and provided all that was needed and much more.

When Winston Churchill, one of England's greatest prime ministers, was a young boy, he attended a private school in England. We probably would think that he was one of the smartest boys in his school, but he was not. In fact, he was in the bottom third of his class. It seemed that he had very little potential even though he was the grandson of Randolph Churchill a british statesman. Instead of giving up, he kept going forward. He graduated from his private school, entered the university, and then went to military school. Then he served in the British army in India and Africa before becoming prime minister and was one of the masterminds behind the allied victory in Europe during World War II.

Years later, he accepted a speaking engagement at his old school. The day before he arrived, the headmaster called all the students together and told them, "Tomorrow the prime minister is coming to speak. He is the most eloquent man in our country. Therefore, I want you to take very good notes. I don't want you to miss a single word that he has to say because this is going to be one of those once-in-a-lifetime opportunities." Everyone was excited and full of anticipation. When the five-foot five-inch prime minister walked into the hushed auditorium, every eye in the room was focused on him. Finally, after the principal gave a tremendous and beautiful oration about all of Churchill's accomplishments, the prime minister stood up, walked up to the podium, and said these words: "Gentlemen, never give up! Never give up! Never give up! Never, never, never, never!" Then he walked back to his chair and sat down.

There is never a time when God gives up on us. His eternal hope is ours, and He gives us the faith we need to hold out during seasons of great difficulty. Moses endured as one seeing God. When we learn to do the same, temptation may come, but we will not yield to its pull. Put your faith, hope, and trust in God. Do not look at your circumstances. Commit yourself to doing what He requires of you. Cling to the promises in His Word. Then when desperation pulls at your heart, you can cry out to Him, knowing that He hears your every word and will answer and provide the encouragement you need to hold out in the face of adversity.

CHAPTER 3

God Has an Answer for Your Need

When the world around you is unraveling, it is hard to imagine being still and trusting God. Yet this is exactly what He wants us to do. In Luke, Jesus comforts those who are worried about the future. "Do not be afraid, little flock, for your Father has chosen gladly to give you the kingdom" (12:32). By accepting Christ as their Savior, they already had a place secured for them in heaven. Therefore, they did not need to worry about the circumstances surrounding their lives. Jesus assured them,

> If God so clothes the grass in the field, which is alive today and tomorrow is thrown into the furnace, how much more will He clothe you? You men of little faith! And do not seek what you will eat and what you will drink, and do not keep worrying. For all these things the nations of the world eagerly seek; but your Father knows that you need these things. But seek His kingdom, and these things will be added to you. (Luke 12:28–31)

Just as these words brought comfort to those who heard the Savior say them, they are a source of comfort today because they remind us that God is not distant and has not forgotten His promises to us. He is a personal God who is aware of every need we have. He also knows when these needs should be addressed. Many people today spend a great deal of time worrying about the future. The news media does their part in fueling the unrealistic fears of those who stay glued to their televisions. Their eyes become focused on predictions and events that have nothing to do with God's amazing ability to provide for His children.

The Reasons for Problems and Trials

When was the last time you heard a news reporter look directly into the camera and remind you to trust God and believe in His ability to provide for the needs you have? More than likely, this will never happen during today's news programs! This is because we are living in a world that is not operating according to God's principles. Therefore, each morning as we get up, we need to put on His armor as Paul outlined in Ephesians 6, and we need to set aside some time to read His Word and pray. Far too often, people get up, rush to put on the coffee, and then turn on the television to see what is happening in the world. I can tell you that what you will hear 90 percent of the time will be negative. Satan is the prince of this world, and he definitely influences what is broadcast each day.

The enemy may try to deceive us into thinking that he is in control but this is nonsense. God is the One who has final control. He is infinite in wisdom and knowledge. He knows all things. Anything that touches our lives has to pass through Him before it gets to us. Nothing happens without His full knowledge. And nothing is too great or too small for Him to handle. The very fact that the check you thought would come on Monday has not arrived concerns Him, but there are times when He allows us to wait for His answer a little longer than we would choose. The fact is: God allows problems and difficulty for several reasons.

Our priorities get out of line, and He wants to show us how to readjust them. Jesus told His followers, "Do not worry about your life" (Luke 12:22). However, many of the people did not know He was the Messiah. Therefore, they believed they had a good reason to become worried. They lived in a time that was full of turmoil. The Roman government kept a tight rule on their lives, and it was hard to make a good living. The taxes were high, and the political oppression was great. Certainly, many of us can identify with the needs these people had, but Jesus is the Prince of Peace. One of His first goals in coming to earth was to offer peace to our tired and troubled hearts and minds.

Instead of worrying and becoming fretful about our circumstances, He wants us to place our trust in Him and allow Him to interject His peace and assurance into our circumstances. Today, many people are living lives that are far from what God planned for them. They are entrapped by sin and spend most of their time trying to justify the lifestyle they have chosen. True peace cannot come to the person who has not surrendered his or her life to the Lord. We can try to make the broken pieces fit, but they never will until our hearts are fully His.

God is never out of control no matter how dark or stormy life becomes. After all, the birds of the air never toil or worry. They don't frantically wonder what they will eat. Instead, they will get up each day with the understanding that they will have what they need. In this passage in Luke, Jesus is simply saying that if this is true for the most insignificant animal, then it is certainly true for you and me—people who were created in His image and for His fellowship and glory.

God allows adversity to touch our lives so that we will turn to Him. Nothing gets our attention any quicker than adversity. Nothing has the power to threaten our sense of peace and joy the way tribulation does. Many times, God uses difficulty and heartache to draw us back to Him and to make us aware of His intimate love. He enjoys our company and wants to build a personal relationship with us. Perhaps you have drifted spiritually and no longer take time to pray and worship Him. This may not have been the case a few years ago when you were a younger Christian. In fact, you prayed, read your Bible, and were overcome with joy at the many ways He was working in your life. However, as you began to grow in your faith, you became distracted by Satan's lie telling you that you really did not have to seek God in trivial matters.

Instead, you think you can make decisions on your own. This is when you began to drift in your devotion to Him. Before you knew it, you were operating in your own strength—doing whatever you felt would be right and not considering God's specific plan for your life. Problems began to grow, and soon you were weary and confused, not knowing which way to turn. The distance that has grown between you and Him may seem many miles wide, but it is not. He is just waiting for you to call out to Him. When you do, He will answer. A primary reason God permits adversity is to draw you back to Himself—close to His side because He loves you and knows that if you keep going, you will experience even greater heartache and hurt.

God uses adversity to purify us and prepare us for greater service. When he was sixteen, David was anointed king of Israel. He was not afraid to demonstrate His love and loyalty to the Lord. In fact, he wrote most of the book of Psalms. Yet David spent years waiting to assume the position God had given him. Why did it take so long for the Lord to clear the way for him? One of the reasons is this: we learn some of our greatest lessons in times of adversity. This is where God sifts us for service and purifies us for the work He wants us to do. When it comes to playing the piano, even those who truly are gifted with this talent must spend hours practicing scales and going over the material they will perform. The same is true in the area of sports. Gifted athletes spend many hours in strenuous and difficult training. Because of the commitment and effort involved, many people give up before they achieve their goals.

They fail to see how difficulty and hardship are preparing them for the blessings that will ultimately come their way.

God uses adversity to conform us to His image. In times of deep sorrow, it can be hard to imagine how the sun will ever shine again. You never will have God's infinite knowledge, but you can learn to think like Him by reading and studying His Word. Tragedies like category five hurricanes come and go in a matter of days, but the aftermath lingers for months and even years. In fact, three years after Hurricane Andrew swept over the southern tip of Florida, the destruction was still evident. Countless houses remained abandoned and uninhabitable.

The effects of a loved one's death, a difficult divorce, and sudden disappointment can linger for a long time, causing us to doubt ourselves and also the goodness of God. We must maintain a strong relationship with Him and with other believers who know how to encourage and motivate us to keep going. When the disciples thought their lives were about to end, they cried out in hopelessness. They were certain that all was lost. Maybe you have felt this same way. One day, life seemed bright and even perfect; then suddenly a storm erupted, and you fell into hopeless despair.

When they pushed away from the shoreline and raised their sails, no one was thinking about having to face adversity. Jesus had sent them on ahead with the promise that He would join them later. As they settled down in the boat and talked about the day's activities, they may have noticed a chilling wind beginning to blow. Still, no one became alarmed until they looked up and saw the thick, dark clouds building overhead. F. B. Meyer tells us, "A storm is the outskirts of [God's] robe, the symptom of His advent, the environment of His presence." The disciples certainly would testify to this. Crossing over the Sea of Galilee one evening, they encountered a swift and intense storm. Strong storms here were common, and these men were seasoned fishermen. In fact, Peter probably had weathered many storms on his own, but this was different, and all three men began to question if they would survive.

Finally, they called out to the Lord—the only One who could really help them (Matt. 8:25). Jesus was asleep in the bow of the boat. When they woke Him, He immediately stood up and commanded the waves and the winds to be still. Then He turned to them and asked, "Why are you afraid, you men of little faith?" (v. 26). Was He unaware of their circumstances? No. He knew exactly what they were facing, just as He knows what you are facing at this very minute. These men were in God's classroom. They were learning what it meant to trust Him entirely—no matter how threatening the winds and waves of adversity appeared.

God allows adversity so that we may experience His comfort. What is the first step you take when disappointment strikes? Do you turn and drop to your knees in prayer seeking God's wisdom, or do you pick up the telephone and quickly call a friend to ask advice about how you should handle the event? Without a doubt, the first thing we should do is turn to the Lord in prayer. This is true for times of difficulty as well as times when we feel great joy. God wants to comfort us in our sorrow just as He wants to celebrate with us when we have experienced an answer to our prayers. In times of adversity, we also have an opportunity to comfort others who are suffering. Jesus Christ is the God of all comfort. Just as the good Samaritan cared for the man who had been attacked by a band of robbers, Jesus Christ will care for you in an even greater way (Luke 10:30–37). He binds up your broken heart, and though the storm clouds may rest over your life for some time, He does not abandon you.

The storms of life reveal the depth of our convictions. After Christ's death, the disciples were in shock. They could not believe that Jesus had been crucified. Fear gripped their hearts, and they fled thinking that they also would be arrested. The Lord predicted Peter's denial, but the disciple did not believe that he would deny the Savior. However, he did—not once, but three times! In the aftermath of the storm, Peter tried to understand what had gone wrong and why it had happened. He was looking at Christ's death from a human perspective and not with God's will in mind. His denial of the Savior came as a result of wanting to protect himself. Instead of standing firm on his convictions that Jesus was the Son of God, Peter said that he did not even know Him.

As the winds of adversity threatened His very life, Peter realized what he had done and cried out to God. His denial had caused an emotional agony unlike anything he had experienced. The mental pain that came from being separated from the Lord was horrendous. Not only was Jesus his Savior, He also was Peter's friend. Three days later, Christ arose from the grave. And even in the glory of His resurrection, He did not forget Peter. God sent an angel to the women who had gathered at the tomb. He said to them, "Do not be amazed; you are looking for Jesus the Nazarene, who has been crucified. He has risen; He is not here; behold, here is the place where they laid Him. But go, tell His disciples and *Peter,* 'He is going ahead of you to Galilee; there you will see Him, just as He told you'" (Mark 16:6–7, emphasis added). The angel included Peter because God knew his heart. His plan for Peter's life was not derailed by the disciple's denial. When we are weak, God is strong (1 Cor. 4:10). And when we stand on the convictions we have in Christ, then we will be able to weather the storms of life—not in our strength, but in His.

Adversity can signal an oncoming change. Saul was totally convinced his persecution of Christians was right on track. He watched with approval as Stephen was stoned to death, even to the point of holding the robes of the individuals who took part in the attack. He cheered them on and in doing so drew God's wrathful attention. A short time later, the Lord struck him blind with a light on the Damascus road. In a split second, Paul went from being a man who was breathing threats against the followers of Christ to a person who was completely humble in the presence of God. His human blindness was a doorway to spiritual insight. Suddenly, he knew that Jesus was Lord, and all he wanted to do was serve Him. God uses adversity to get our attention and redirect our lives. In that short moment, Saul of Tarsus became Paul, a committed follower of the Lord Jesus Christ. His eyesight was restored, but he never forgot the time He saw Jesus. His life was no longer infused with hatred; it was filled with the desire to love God and to be loved by Him. He was captivated by Christ and immediately set out to tell others about the saving grace of the Savior.

When problems come and you do not understand why, ask the Lord, "What are You saying to me? Do You want to reshape something in my life? Are You purifying me for a purpose, redirecting me for a reason?" God always will make His way through the storm clear to you. You may not understand why the clouds have appeared, but you can trust the One who has allowed them to gather. God never wastes our sorrows. Whatever you are facing today, you can be sure that He will use it in some dramatic way tomorrow to bring glory to Himself and to bless you.

CHAPTER 4

The Faith to Stand

There are two passages of scripture that God has used over and over again in my life. The first one is Proverbs 3:5–6: "Trust in the LORD with all your heart and do not lean on your own understanding. In all your ways acknowledge Him, and He will make your paths straight." God placed this scripture in my heart at the very beginning of my Christian life. It also is one that I come back to often because it reminds me that He knows exactly where I am and what I am facing, and that if I will allow Him, He will lead me to the place that I need to be.

The second scripture that God has used as an anchor to my heart during times of adversity is one that we mentioned earlier, Psalm 62. I love the New King James version of this psalm.

Truly my soul silently waits for God;
From Him comes my salvation.
He only is my rock and my salvation;
He is my defense;

I shall not be greatly moved. . . .
My soul, wait silently for God alone,
For my expectation is from Him.
He only is my rock and my salvation;
He is my defense;
I shall not be moved.
In God is my salvation and my glory;
The rock of my strength,
And my refuge, is in God.
Trust in Him at all times, you people;
Pour out your heart before Him;
God is a refuge for us.

(vv. 1–2, 5–8)

All of us will face stormy times—seasons when problems come, many times without warning. This is when we know that we need practical solutions that work. I believe David was in the middle of a very stormy season when he wrote this psalm. When he was about sixteen years old, Samuel the prophet anointed him king of Israel. However, he did not take Israel's throne until he was thirty years old, and that happened only after he waited all those years. During this time of his life, he faced one difficult situation after another.

Most people's idea of waiting is to just sit around doing nothing, but this is *not* what the Bible means when it speaks of waiting upon the Lord. From God's perspective, *waiting* is an action verb. This means it is alive with faith. During difficult times, we must trust God to bring us through the problem, trial, or tragedy. We may think that we are not gaining ground, but we are. In fact, from His viewpoint, we are gaining the most important ground because we are learning to trust Him in the darkest moments of our lives.

One of the greatest benefits that comes from difficulty is an opportunity to draw closer to God and to develop a deeper faith in Him. A second benefit is an intimate relationship with Jesus Christ. There are many things in life that you can purchase with money, but you cannot buy intimacy with God. This comes as a direct result of learning to wait in faith for Him to work on your behalf. Isaiah writes, "Those who wait for the LORD will gain new strength; they will mount up with wings like eagles, they will run and not get tired, they will walk and not become weary" (Isa. 40:31). In this passage, the word *wait* also denotes faithful activity, where we exercise our trust in God even though we may not immediately see any results. Instead of giving in to thoughts of hopelessness and fear, we can keep watch for God's deliverance and guidance.

Waiting for His best means you are willing to remain right where you are until you sense Him leading you on to the next step. It is an act of obedience, which always leads to blessing. This is why it involves faith. I remember different times in my life when I have discussed waiting upon the Lord with other people—friends, pastors, and staff members. After a few days of waiting and trusting God for an answer, they would say, "Why are you waiting? Don't you think we need to keep going? Isn't that what faith is all about—moving forward in difficult and unsure times?" There are times when God will indicate almost immediately that we need to step forward and keep moving. However, at other times, it is crucial to wait for His leading because He knows His plan for our lives. If we move without His guidance, we could miss His best and also end up missing a greater blessing.

Look for His Guidance

Moving forward without His guidance can have disastrous results. In fact, this is how many people end up in deep financial trouble. They make poor decisions financially, and when the bottom drops out, they panic. Instead of entering into a season of prayer where they seek God's will for their lives, they push forward thinking that they need to make some type of decision. But without God's wisdom, they run the risk of falling even deeper into debt. When trouble comes and you do not have God's clear guidance, this is your cue to stop and wait for Him to show you the next move. How does He do this? God speaks to us in three different ways.

Through His Word

The Bible is our greatest source of guidance and direction. It also is His greatest form of communication to us. Within the pages of the Bible, we are given answers to every situation we face. Nothing is left out. If you are discouraged, God has a cure and you will find it in His Word. The same is true for problems with money, relationships, future decisions, and much more. The key to finding the answer to your greatest need is taking time to get alone with God and asking Him to reveal His will for your life through His Word. You can count on this: if you will pray and ask Him to guide you through the challenge you are facing, He will do it. He also will provide the encouragement you need to live each day victoriously and not in defeat and failure. He wants you to be a success, and the first step in this direction is taking time to read and study His Word—His personal Word to you.

Through the Holy Spirit

Once we accept Christ as our Savior, the Holy Spirit comes to live within us. We do not receive part of Him; we receive all there is, and He is our greatest source of comfort, hope, encouragement, and guidance for troubled times. As we read God's Word, the Holy Spirit gives us the ability to retain what we have studied. Then when trouble comes, we will hear His voice speaking words of direction and courage to our hearts. After the sudden death of her husband, Catherine Marshall tells how she remained in the room with his body for a few minutes. She wanted to say a last goodbye. She writes,

> Shivering, I rose to leave the room. I knew that this would be the last time on this earth that I would look upon my husband's face . . . Now there was nothing to do but walk out. I

sensed that out beyond the door, out beyond the chilly hospital corridor, a new life awaited me. That was the last thing in the world I wanted. But then, Peter had not wanted a new life either—not yet anyway—not at just 46. And already he had embarked on that other adventure.

Two paces from the door, I was stopped as by an invisible hand. As I paused, a message was spoken with emphasis and clarity, not audibly, but with the peculiar authority I had come to recognize as the Lord's own voice: Surely goodness and mercy shall follow you all the days of your life.

It was His personal pledge to me and to a son who would now sorely miss his father. (*Meeting God at Every Turn* © 1980 Guidepost edition)

God always goes out before us. We never go alone, and He always prepares the way even when that way is dark and stormy.

Through Trusted Christian Friends or a Pastor

Another way God speaks to us is through the counsel of trusted Christian friends or our pastor. God uses people to encourage, admonish, and offer suggestions. Always make sure that what you hear lines up with God's Word. Many times, well-meaning friends will offer counsel, but it is not God's best for us. Also, we should resist the urge to have our desires validated. In other words, if you know what you are doing is not in keeping with God's will for your life, then asking others to support your effort is dead wrong. Most of the time, we know the way God wants us to go, but if it involves sacrifice or personal surrender, we can become resistant and even disobedient. Psalm 32:9 admonishes us to not become "as the horse or as the mule which have no understanding, whose trappings include bit and bridle to hold them in check." Instead, God instructs us to listen for His voice, and be quick to respond in obedience. "I will instruct you and teach you in the way which you should go; I will counsel you with My eye upon you" (Ps. 32:8).

CHAPTER 5

Wait for God's Timing

In the previous chapters, we have been talking about the importance of waiting on the Lord. Most of God's servants had to wait for His timing and solution to their situations. Job learned to wait. Joseph waited, and David did the same. Many times, this is exactly what God wants us to learn to do—wait for His direction, His call, His plan, and His word to us. But learning to wait during a stormy time also includes something else—learning how to rest in God's presence. When tragedy comes, many times our first response is to tell someone else. This also is true when we receive good news. So often, we reach for the telephone and think of those we can call. However, what would happen if before we dialed the number, we stopped and said, "Lord, I don't understand what I am facing. Will You show me how You want me to respond?" Or, "Thank You, Lord, for providing for me. I did not know how I would make it through to the end of the month, but You knew, and You have given me Your very best."

The woman in Luke 8 had struggled with a terrible illness

for twelve years. She was not only demoralized, she was entrapped in what seemed to be an endless sea of hopelessness. She had spent all her money—all that she owned—on trying to find a cure for her illness. Because of her constant bleeding, she was viewed as unclean and one to be avoided. Not only did her suffering bring physical pain, it also brought tremendous emotional distress and an inescapable sense of loneliness. But God heard her cry for mercy, and He knew exactly when her healing would take place. He knew her by name, and He also realized that in desperation, she would seek the Savior and reach out to touch the very edge of His robe. When faced with a severe trial, many of us do what this woman did—we run first to one person and then to another until we think we have found the help we need. But nothing apart from God works for long. Finally, when we are exhausted and near a point where we want to give up, we cry out to Him and confess our need. This is when we discover that He has been beside us all the time, waiting for us to turn to Him. When this woman touched His robe, she was healed physically, but more than that, she was healed spiritually and emotionally.

According to Jewish tradition, Jesus never should have stopped to talk with this woman. The fact that she was bleeding made her unclean, and yet He told her that her faith had healed her (Luke 8:48). The brokenness of your life does not prevent the Savior from loving you. He loves you and wants to heal the hurt and sorrow that you are facing, and He wants you to know that He has a plan for your life that goes beyond the hurt and frustration you are feeling. He knows what has happened.

He realizes the devastating effects adversity can have on your life, but He also wants you to know that He is not powerless. He will move on your behalf and bring you to a point of peace and rest where you will be able to sense His presence and know that He is in control of all that is beyond your human ability.

Steps to Learning How to Wait

How do you rest when everything within you is hurting and struggling to make sense out of what appears to be a senseless situation?

Ask God to help you understand whether the adversity you are facing is from Him or from Satan. The apostle Paul suffered greatly, but it was not because of any sin that he committed. His suffering was for a greater purpose. At Lystra, he was stoned, left for dead by his enemies, and later abandoned by many who had once worked alongside him. However, in 2 Corinthians 12, he tells us, "Because of the surpassing greatness of the revelations, for this reason, to keep me from exalting myself, there was given me a thorn in the flesh, a messenger of Satan to torment me—to keep me from exalting myself! Concerning this I implored the Lord three times that it might leave me. And He has said to me, 'My grace is sufficient for you, for power is perfected in weakness'" (vv. 7–9). The Person behind the adversity—not the person who created the pain, but the One who used it for His glory—was God.

Joseph's brothers threw him into a pit that was designed to trap wild animals. When a band of traveling merchants came by, they pulled him from the pit and sold him. Later, these merchants sold him as a slave in Egypt. God, however, was with him, and even in a dark and lonely prison cell, the Lord prospered him in spite of his circumstances. When he first landed in prison, he was not ready for the future that God had in mind for him (Gen. 39). It was only through years of captivity that he was trained to be a godly ruler. The time of isolation also kindled within him a fire of compassion and forgiveness. When you have faced severe adversity, you are much more ready to forgive, accept, and love than if you have never tasted the effects of sorrow and disappointment. When Joseph's brothers came to Egypt asking to buy grain, he was positioned by God to help them and ended up being the key to their survival. He never could have been ready for such a task had he not been trained at the hands of adversity. You may be wondering why such difficulty has come into your life. However, the greater question is, "Lord, how do You plan to use this difficulty so I may serve You better?"

Be willing to submit to God's time frame. Many times when difficulty comes, Satan tempts us to think that we need to escape the problem. He tells us that we do not have to listen to our manager at work, our husband or wife, or anyone we see as an authority figure. Pride is the key reason Satan was cast out of heaven. The apostle Peter makes it clear that we are to be people of submission. He writes, "You younger men, likewise, be subject to your elders; and all of you, clothe yourselves with humility toward one another, for God is opposed to the proud, but gives grace to the humble. Therefore humble yourselves under the mighty hand of God, that He may exalt you at the proper time, casting all your anxiety on Him, because He cares for you" (1 Pet. 5:5–7).

If we are wise, when adversity hits, we will immediately ask the Lord to give us His wisdom and to show us how we need to respond to the trial. Often He wants us to humble ourselves before Him and trust Him to work in our circumstances. But the world views humility and submission as being positions of weakness. However, this is not God's view. When we submit ourselves to His plan—even if it includes trial and heartache—we position ourselves for tremendous blessing. Joseph submitted to God's plan, and the result of his obedience was tremendous! He was never irate or bitter. He never vowed to destroy his brothers or seek revenge on those who betrayed him. When all was exposed, he realized what he already knew: God had a plan and a purpose in mind for his life, and all he had to do was to be willing to follow the course and obey the One who could bring deliverance to his life. All adversity that comes into the life of a believer must be sifted through the permissive will of God. As we said earlier, He allows difficulty for a purpose. Usually, it is to bring glory to Himself, draw us closer to Him, redirect our lives, test the depth of our faith, or strengthen us for a greater purpose. In times of extreme darkness, it is very important to remember that God is always at work. We may not see the evidence, but He is active and He knows exactly what to do so that we have His best in the future.

Therefore, when trouble hits, resist the urge to focus on yourself, your ambition, and personal desires. Instead, focus on God by realizing that He knows all about the sorrows you are facing, and He has promised to take each one and change it into a moment of eternal value. His viewpoint of adversity is not one of hopelessness and setback. Instead, it is one of spiritual advancement. "He who searches the hearts knows what the mind of the Spirit is, because He intercedes for the saints according to the will of God. And we know that God causes all things to work together for good to those who love God, to those who are called according to His purpose" (Rom. 8:27–28).

Know that there is a time limit to suffering. Nothing is forever, and no sorrow we face is wasted in God's eyes. There was a time limit set for Joseph's suffering. The same was true in David's life, just as it is with us. You may have spent the past year wondering if you will ever be able to live a normal life again. The answer is yes and also no. If we allow God to carry us through times of adversity, we will be changed in ways we never thought possible. A new depth and dimension will be added to our lives. What we once viewed as being normal will be replaced by something that bears a greater value because it comes to us in the image of the Lord Jesus Christ. This changes us and makes us more sensitive to God and to those around us who are hurting. Because adversity has the ability to purge us of thoughts and actions that are not in keeping with God's principles, we also find that our thoughts have changed. We no longer think about going back to the place we were before adversity touched our lives. While it is hard to leave the memory of a loved one behind, we realize that life is worth living, and we must live so that Christ can live through us.

No one who has ever loved deeply and then lost that love wants to move on immediately. But in time, and with God's help, that person understands that God's plan for his or her life is not over; it is just taking a different path than the one he or she thought would be traveled. When we realize that God is healing and restoring our hearts, we want to move on and even farther than we have gone before. David did take the throne of Israel, and Joseph became ruler over all of Egypt—only Pharaoh was greater in power. Most of the time when trouble comes, we do not immediately ask, "What will be the beneficial outcome?" Instead, we struggle with feelings of regret and wonder if we could have done something to prevent it, or we become angry. We do not see how God can use our trouble to bring blessing and hope in our lives through a greater faith in God. Tragedy strikes, and we cry out, "Why, God?"

God tells us, "My thoughts are not your thoughts, nor are your ways My ways" (Isa. 55:8). We may not understand why our suffering lingers or the reason the trial we are facing does not let up, but God knows. And if we will trust Him in the midst of it, He will bring us through to a place of blessing. When all hope appears to be gone, God always makes a way for us to travel. When you come to your last paycheck and wonder how you will pay the next bill, He knows, and He is our sufficiency for every need we have. The apostle Paul writes, "God is able to make all grace abound to you, so that always having all sufficiency in everything, you may have an abundance for every good deed" (2 Cor. 9:8). There is no need to doubt the goodness of God. He is ever faithful, and we can trust Him to provide exactly what we need when we need it.

Are you looking at your circumstances and becoming more fearful by the minute, or are you resting in the fact that God has promised to provide for every need you have—completely and perfectly and on time (Phil. 4:19)? He has never failed to keep a single promise, and no matter what you are facing, He has an answer for your greatest need when you turn to Him and place your complete trust in Him. Therefore, "Be anxious for nothing, but in everything by prayer and supplication with thanksgiving let your requests be made known to God. And the peace of God, which surpasses all comprehension, will guard your hearts and your minds in Christ Jesus" (Phil. 4:6–7). God wants to make a way through the darkness you are facing. He wants to help you solve the problem that is holding you back from being the very best you can be. The question is, are you willing to wait for His timing, and will you follow where He leads?

CHAPTER 6

A Change in Attitude

The apostle Paul probably thought long and hard about the words God had spoken to him. During a time when most of us would have given up, Paul remained strong in his faith because he had God's promise: "My grace is sufficient for you, for power is perfected in weakness" (2 Cor. 12:9).

The adversity you are facing may seem far too great for you to handle, but it is not for God. You wonder how you will make it through another day. Your nights are long, and your days filled with thoughts of anxiety and even fear as you wonder, *Where is God? Why doesn't He stop this pain? Didn't He promise to provide for all my needs?* God has not forgotten His promises to you. The same God who promised to take care of the apostle Paul will, indeed, take care of you (Phil. 4:19). However, just like Paul, God wants you to gain a new perspective on adversity. In fact, He may want to adjust your attitude toward hardship and trouble. You may think that the men and women in the Bible never doubted God and certainly were never fearful, but this is not true.

Each one faced many temptations. Just like us, they became frightened and cried out to God for help and wisdom to know how to handle the situations facing them. Their lives were etched with moments of adversity and trials because both of these are useful in developing spiritual character and loving devotion to God.

A Greater Purpose

When God allows a problem or adversity to linger, we can be sure that something good is about to happen. We also can choose to approach adversity in one of two ways. We can sink into discouragement, or we can trust God to lead us through the difficulty and on to greater blessing. Here is the catch: God may not immediately change our circumstances. In fact, He may allow the adversity to continue to strengthen and purify our faith. One young man who had been out of work for several months was quick to ask, "Why doesn't God open up some opportunity for me? I've prayed, but He seems so quiet. What should I do?" Just because we do not see the immediate evidence of God's work in our lives does not mean He has stopped working. God is always at work. The news we hoped to receive may be delayed but His promises are true. At the right time, He will fulfill each one. Everything comes down to this: Do we truly believe God is in control of our circumstances? If we do, will we trust Him for the outcome? Often people get into serious trouble because they do not have the right view of adversity and problems. When a problem comes, instead of allowing God to solve it, they strain hard against the oars, fearing they will lose their lives. Many times, God wants us to take a step of faith, but not without His guidance. It takes a fraction of a second for God to tell you to turn this way or another way. However, when your mind is full of thoughts about what you should or should not do, you will not be able to hear His voice. Paul could have spent lots of time and energy seeking help and advice from others, but he knew he already had the greatest source of help in Jesus Christ. The delay or lack of an answer meant that there had to be something that God wanted him to learn and experience.

God never wastes our sorrows. He has a plan in mind for every problem and frustration we face. Always remember, He is not the One who created the adversity, but He uses it to strengthen our faith and mold our lives so that we reflect His love and grace to others. It is in the hard places in life that we learn the deeper truths of God. Paul struggled with his adversity for a long time. However, he began to understand exactly why God allowed it. Years before, he had a spiritual experience with the Lord that changed his life. It opened his eyes to a depth of God's majesty that few people come to know. This one event could have left him feeling smug and prideful. The thorn that Satan sent his way was allowed by God to buffet him so that he would not become proud but would remain a humble man who worshiped Christ above all else. This painful adversity made Paul keenly sensitive to God's will and purpose for his life.

The Key to Facing Your Problems Victoriously

The key to understanding adversity is found by asking God to make you sensitive to why He has allowed this in your life. Paul asked the Lord to remove the difficulty he was facing, and you can too. But the greater blessing comes in learning what God has for you to learn. Never be afraid of what He will show you, because He knows adversity and trials are doors to future blessings. The apostle may have suffered greatly, but God used him mightily. Out of the furnace of affliction came a tremendous testimony of faith. More than half of the New Testament was written by the apostle Paul. You may be tempted to say, "How can this be true? The problem I am facing has changed everything." Don't discount God. He knows the depth of your heartache, and He is working to bring you to a new place—a place of hope and extreme blessing. If the problem has come as a result of something you have or have not done, then God also will make this clear. Once you admit your sin, He is quick to forgive and restore your broken fellowship with Him. He also provides the wisdom and comfort you need to get through the adversity. He is the God of all comfort. He heals the brokenhearted and binds up their wounds (Isa. 61:1). "Grace to you," writes the apostle Paul, "and peace from God our Father and the Lord Jesus Christ. Blessed be the God and Father of our Lord Jesus Christ, the Father of mercies and God of all comfort, who comforts us in all our affliction" (2 Cor. 1:2–4).

Many people do not live with an eternal mind-set. They live for today and for themselves without considering what God wants them to do. They are earthbound in their thoughts and have not lifted up their eyes to the Lord to see His glory and goodness being poured out for them. Paul did, however. Therefore, when suffering came, he realized God had a plan for it in his life. He did not give up, nor did his faith buckle—and we also can remain faithful and strong in our love for the Savior.

God is aware of the trial you are facing. He cares for you or He would not allow disappointment to come your way. Does this sound odd? It should not, because just like an athlete preparing for a great competition, we are being trained to serve and honor God with our lives. He wants to teach us to be people of compassion—people who love and pray for those who have hurt us. While He never takes pleasure in our heartaches, He uses whatever problem or adversity we face to draw us closer to Him. Perhaps you are going through a very dark valley. You feel as though you are alone and do not know what will come your way next. You want to believe God is aware of your circumstances, but there is a question residing in the back of your mind. *Does He really care?*

Paul would answer with a resounding yes! Peter would agree; he reminds us to "humble yourselves under the mighty hand of God, that He may exalt you at the proper time, casting all your anxiety on Him, because He cares for you" (1 Pet. 5:6–7). The word *humble* is a call to become like Jesus Christ in times of suffering. Humility is not weakness. Instead, it reflects a great and unending strength—the same strength we have in God's Son who died on the cross for our sins and salvation. Speaking of His life, Paul writes, "When I am weak, then I am strong" (2 Cor. 12:10). The strength that both Peter and Paul are talking about is not a self-induced strength. It is a God-directed strength that comes when we humble ourselves before God. This means that we bow down and submit our lives to Christ, trusting Him to take care of every problem and difficulty we have.

James agrees with Peter and Paul. He admonishes those who receive his letter to "consider it all joy, my brethren, when you encounter various trials, knowing that the testing of your faith produces endurance. And let endurance have its perfect result, so that you may be perfect and complete, lacking in nothing" (James 1:2–4). The theme James uses to open his letter is one of submission to suffering. This does not mean giving up and giving in, but standing firm in your faith even when it appears the odds are completely stacked against you.

When Problems Seem Great!

The fact is, James was writing to a group of people who had lost everything. They were Jewish believers who were forced to leave their homes in and around Jerusalem. Many had been separated from their family and loved ones. Their sorrow was deep, but their hope was alive even though they faced the daily threat of death at the hands of the Roman government. Their problems seemed great, but nothing they faced was greater than God's love for them.

When difficulty comes, we usually get through a few days thinking that God will rescue us. If the trial lingers, then stress builds, and this has the potential to wear on our emotions. Soon, we may catch ourselves wondering if there is any hope for the future. However, there always is hope with Christ—always another opportunity and always enough wisdom and strength to get through the situation victoriously. God knows that each one of us can be tempted to think that our problems and circumstances are far worse than what someone else is facing. When we begin to lift our heads and hearts, we find that many are suffering, and we are not alone in our quest to trust God in difficult and unreasonable times.

How do we change our attitude toward adversity?

Ask God to help you see the problem from His perspective. Many times, He wants to use your problem to teach someone else how to handle difficulty. Most of us would not think of this. But since He is the God of all comfort, He wants us to learn to be comforters too. Apart from trial and tribulation, we cannot do this. Paul learned to identify with the suffering of those in the New Testament church by facing the same, and even greater, fiery trials.

Realize the problem or adversity is being used by God to draw you closer to Him. Your first response to any trial should be to ask, "Lord, what are You trying to teach me through this experience?" Remember, God always sifts every single heartache, sorrow, disappointment, trial, and tribulation so that it fits your life perfectly. He wants the disappointment or frustration to be something that will accomplish His will in your life. When you begin to look at adversity this way—the way God views it—your life will change. Suddenly you will understand as Paul did that God has an eternal purpose in mind for allowing you to face such difficulty. He loves you, and though you feel His discipline in your life, you know that He is creating within you a greater sense of faith, love, and trust. Watchman Nee believed that all the new things we learn about God come as a result of facing adversity. It is in times of deep trial, when our faith is tested beyond our normal ability to endure, that we discover God's loving hand holding us up and reassuring us that He will never leave. He shifts the trial so that it fits His plan for us, and then He surrounds it with His love and grace.

Realize that God never takes our heartaches lightly. He knows the depth of the hurt we suffer. He also understands when we feel as though we cannot continue, but we must. The writer of Hebrews cheers us on as he writes, "Do not throw away your confidence, which has a great reward. For you have need of endurance, so that when you have done the will of God, you may receive what was promised" (10:35–36). The confidence we have is our position before a loving God who has sent His only Son to die on the cross for us. Nothing was fair about the crucifixion. Jesus was falsely accused of crimes He did not commit. However, God had a greater plan in mind for His Son. His death would satisfy the need for our sin's atonement. Not only are we forgiven, we are saved through His grace by the confession of our sin and the profession of our faith in Christ. We can draw near to God and know that He hears our deepest cry for help.

When adversity first strikes, it always seems too difficult to bear. Problems are stressful, sudden tragedies are shocking, and memories of disappointment can linger; but through Christ, we can face all that comes our way, knowing that there is an eternal reason for our suffering and a way to handle the problem. It is God's way. After all, it was His love that allowed His Son to die for you and me on Calvary's cross. The world has known no greater love than this. Therefore,

- Ask Him to help you to respond to the difficulty correctly.
- Pray that you sense His love even though the darkness around you is painful and deep.
- Remain strong in your faith and trust Him fully.

• Be determined that you will not waste your sorrows, but will learn all God desires for you to learn.

Are you prepared to suffer if necessary so others may come to know the grace and love of Christ? Are you willing to support and care for a loved one who is hurting—maybe even dying? Because of God's love that was displayed for you and me on the cross, suffering, blessing, and His eternal love will be forever joined together. We cannot have one without the other.

CHAPTER 7

Solving Problems Through Prayer

Once you became a member of God's family, Satan's personal goal for your life shifted. Because he knows he no longer has power over your soul or eternal destiny—these are in God's care—his focus changes. He moves quickly, hoping to create heartache, frustration, and discouragement within your life. He will stop at nothing to achieve this wretched goal. Why? He wants you to become so sorrowful, angry, and stressed that you grow weary and abandon your faith. However, this is never an option for a true believer.

We are called by God to be overcomers through Jesus (Rom. 8:37). The apostle Paul writes, "I am convinced that neither death, nor life, nor angels, nor principalities, nor things present, nor things to come, nor powers, nor height, nor depth, nor any other created thing, will be able to separate us from the love of God, which is in Christ Jesus our Lord" (Rom. 8:38–39). As we have discussed, God has a reason for the problems we face. However, He also has methods to handle each one. When life takes a sudden turn in a dark direction, we have to make a choice: to trust and obey Him, or to struggle with our fears and doubts on our own. It is always God's desire that we will turn to Him in prayer for wisdom and strength.

Make the Right Choice

In 2 Chronicles, after a series of missteps, King Jehoshaphat found himself and the nation of Judah in a very difficult situation. In fact, the threat facing them was deadly. And for a time, it appeared Judah would be overthrown. The king had tried to "mend fences" with his neighboring enemies—something he should not have done since this only led to more trouble. Instead of soothing enemy forces, the menacing armies devised a plan to march on Jerusalem and destroy it. When King Jehoshaphat received the word of impending danger, fear filled his heart. However, instead of allowing fear to direct and rule his emotions, he did the one thing he knew would bring hope to an otherwise deteriorating situation: he turned to the Lord in prayer. In other words, fear was not his final choice. It came as a quick response to his circumstances, but he did not cling to it. Instead, he responded in faith through prayer. When trouble strikes without warning, what is your first response?

Most of us have had the same type of experience. Suddenly, our lives take a dark and stormy turn. Our minds fill quickly with thoughts of panic, but God's Spirit also rises up within us to remind us that He is in control of even the most chaotic situation. If you forget everything else, remember this: God is always in control. Nothing that comes your way catches Him off guard. He is Lord over every detail of life and certainly over every storm—no matter how deep or dark it becomes.

Learn to Respond Correctly

Jehoshaphat received news that his enemies were plotting against him. He was a righteous king—the king of Judah for nearly twenty-five years. He sought to bring about a revival of faith among God's people. It is believed that he had an army that consisted of close to a million men. However, on this particular occasion, that number seemed very small when compared to the armies of his enemies—the Moabites and the Ammonites. When their plan began to unfold, momentary panic swept over his heart and the hearts of the people. However, he quickly adjusted his thinking by turning to God in prayer: "Then some came and reported to Jehoshaphat, saying, 'A great multitude is coming against you from beyond the sea, out of Aram and behold, they are in Hazazon-tamar (that is Engedi).' Jehoshaphat was afraid and turned his attention to seek the LORD, and proclaimed a fast throughout all Judah" (2 Chron. 20:2–3).

Immediately the king knew there was only one place to

find hope, and that was in God's sovereign care. He recalled what the Lord had done for Israel in the past and knew that God would not abandon the nation now. As we have mentioned in earlier chapters, God has several reasons for allowing us to face difficult situations:

He wants you to trust Him to a greater degree.

He uses adversity to draw us even closer to Him. We look at our problems and think, *How will I ever make it through this?* But God says, "All things are possible for Me" (Mark 10:27).

He wants to demonstrate His faithfulness.

Children learn through repetition, and we do also. If there is a hint of pride in our lives, God will seek to remove it, and usually, the tool He chooses is your adversity. However, if you will trust, you will be delivered from your greatest fear (Ps. 72:12).

He wants to teach you an even greater lesson of faith.

God stretches your faith, but He will not break your heart. Each time a problem comes, He stretches you a little farther. He is watching for the response of your heart. In trying times, remember: "A bruised reed He will not break and a dimly burning wick He will not extinguish" (Isa. 42:3).

He wants you to learn from your mistakes so you will not repeat them.

He disciplines those He loves (Heb. 12:6). He also knows when you need His wisdom concerning a decision that has turned out badly. You may have to suffer the consequences of your wrong choice, but He will provide relief and hope as you trust Him and refuse to become entangled with thoughts of fear and even death. There are times when people try to negotiate their way out of a bad situation. However, there was no escape route for Judah. They were stuck in a very narrow place. But they were not without hope. They had a powerful offensive weapon at their disposal. It is the same weapon that God has given us. It is prayer. When we pray—

- God always listens.
- He is committed to answer our cries for help.
- He views our prayers as a proclamation of faith in Him.
- He moves on our behalf.

Together: Prayer and Might

"So Judah gathered together to seek help from the LORD; they even came from all the cities of Judah to seek the LORD. So Jehoshaphat stood in the assembly of Judah and Jerusalem, in the house of the LORD before the new court, and he said, "O LORD, the God of our fathers, are You not God in the heavens? And are You not ruler over all the kingdoms of the nations? Power and might are in Your hand so that no one can stand against You" (2 Chron. 20:4–6). Devotional prayers are prayers that we say to gain an even greater sense of God's presence surrounding us. Each morning, before we even get out of bed, we need to ask God to order our steps, to make us aware of His closeness and the many ways He seeks to guide us. Later, before we head out to the office or school, or to run errands and meet clients, we need to devote time to be alone with Him in prayer, study, and worship.

Notice that the first thing Judah did was to gather in God's presence. The people wanted to be near Him, and they also wanted Him to know that they needed Him. Their prayer was not devotional; it was a cry for help. However, before they came to this point, they had established a relationship with the Lord. This means that their devotion, though it wavered at times, was set on God. Jehoshaphat had worked to remove many of the pagan high places in the land. He had worked to create an environment of worship to God and none other. Many times, to gain our full attention, God will allow us to face a situation that is far too great for us to handle on our own. We need Him, and this is exactly where Judah was standing—in a place of extreme need and dependence on Him.

The Essentials of Prayer

The next step they took was to readjust their thinking. As long as you believe God will not answer your prayers, He probably won't, but not because He is unwilling. Often, we move out ahead of Him. We may pray and then jump up and think we need to fix the situation. We do not give God a chance, and we certainly do not allow Him time to answer our prayers. Waiting on God is essential to seeing how He will move on your behalf. Many times, He will answer immediately, as we will see by studying this chapter further. Other times, He calls us to wait until He has all the pieces in place to accomplish what He wants to do. You could be dealing with a problem that has lingered for weeks, months, and even years. You may wonder if God really knows what you are facing or if He cares. Waiting is not passive. It is an active step of faith. A person chooses to wait on God because he or she wants the best.

When you and I face challenges in life but we do not think correctly about Him, then any prayer we say will be in vain. You have heard people say, "I have told God about my problem, but nothing has happened. I have prayed and prayed, and He hasn't given me a solution. In fact, I feel worse off. Why doesn't God answer my prayer? Why is He so quiet, especially when He knows that I am hurting and the problem is growing larger every day?"

Jehoshaphat not only prayed, he began to recall all that God had done for the people. "Did You not, O our God, drive out the inhabitants of this land before Your people Israel and give it to the descendants of Abraham Your friend forever?" (2 Chron. 20:7). The king wanted to make sure that God remembered that He was the One who brought His people to this point. He had protected them, and now they were facing a horrendous threat—one that could undo all that the Lord had done. There will be times in your life when you will face situations at work or in service at your church when you will feel as though all that you have gained on a project could be lost as a result of another's selfish actions. Judah's enemies wanted to dominate and overthrow them because they worshiped the living God. It is very simple. Some may argue that there was material spoil to be gained, but what was really at stake was God's ability to protect and provide for those He loved.

Right Focus, Right Thinking

Right focus and right thinking always yield right results. Therefore, if you will follow the next few steps, I guarantee you that God will deal with the problem that you are facing. He will provide a solution. But first, the question you must answer is, am I willing to abide by God's solution—regardless of what that solution entails? If you come to God in prayer with a preconceived notion of what the solution needs to look like, then you will be disappointed. There may be times when God motivates you to pray a certain way. This is certainly evident in the prayer that Jehoshaphat prayed. God led him to recall the ways He had worked in the past to create an atmosphere of hope and courage among the people.

Why would you pray the following and expect God to act: "Lord, I don't know how You will help me. I feel so weak and helpless. I can't feel Your love. Have You left me?" God stands firmly beside you as you pray. He has never failed you, and He never will. If you refuse to trust Him, you will face times of disappointment and defeat. However, if you will believe in Him—trust Him no matter how deep the valley becomes—He will lift you up and bring you safely through the difficulty. There are several things we need to learn to pray with faith and power. These are always true and need to be applied to your heart and life.

God is interested in your problem. Jehoshaphat prayed, "LORD, the God of our fathers, are You not God in the heavens? . . . Are you not ruler over all the kingdoms of the nation?" (2 Chron. 20:6). He was reminding himself and those who heard his prayer that there was no one as great and as faithful as the Lord God. The people knew God had led them out of Egypt and brought them to this point. But their minds needed to be reset—refocused—on the Lord. They could not move another step without Him because He was over all things. There are times when we need to take this same step. The answer to our prayers may seem evident. The solution to our problems can only be solved one way, and that is God's way. However, emotions such as fear, doubt, disbelief, and even deep sorrow can cloud our faith and diminish our trust in Him.

God has made a commitment to you. The moment you pray and ask Him to come into your life and save you from your sins, He does just that. He saves you from eternal death and establishes an eternal covenant with you that can never be broken. Your personal relationship with the Savior begins the moment you accept what He did for you on Calvary's cross as payment for your sins. He died and paid the penalty of your transgressions. Three days later, He rose and ascended to the heavenly Father's right hand, where He makes constant intercession on your behalf (Heb. 7:25). Whatever need you have, Jesus is committed to asking the Father to provide it for you.

Imagine the God of the universe, who is not only aware of your needs but longs to meet each one and give you the desires of your heart. Through salvation, you become a member of the family of God. As His son or daughter, this relationship is irrevocable. Your joys, heartaches, and problems also belong to God. The same was true for the nation of Judah. God was with them. Actually, He was the Commander over all that took place the day they marched into battle.

The next thing you need to remember is something we have stated earlier. *No problem is too big for Him to handle.* He is greater than any sorrow or disappointment you will ever face. You may be having a difficult time at work. Your boss is pressing you to perform with greater speed and accuracy in a much shorter length of time. The stress is overwhelming, and you know that you cannot quit because you have monthly bills that are due.

There are times when He allows a situation to get out of control to show us He is over all things. If the armies mounting an attack against Jehoshaphat had gathered but then became afraid and disbanded, more than likely the people of Judah would have become proud. They would have celebrated instead of turning to the Lord in prayer. Whatever drives you to God is good for you. This is because it reveals your weaknesses, your inability to handle life apart from Him, and your need for Him. Faced with a very serious physical problem, the apostle Paul writes,

Concerning this I implored the Lord three times that it might leave me. And He has said to me, "My grace is sufficient for you, for power is perfected in weakness." Most gladly, therefore, I will rather boast about my weaknesses, so that the power of Christ may dwell in me.

Therefore I am well content with weaknesses, with insults, with distresses, with persecutions, with difficulties, for Christ's sake; for when I am weak, then I am strong. (2 Cor. 12:8–10)

The implication of Paul's words is this: "When I am weak—emotionally, physically, or spiritually—then I am made strong through faith in Jesus Christ." Strength does not come through human ability to solve difficult issues; it comes through personal surrender—first to Him and then to the situation He has allowed to come into your life. In order to gain the victory, you must allow Him to take control of all that concerns you. When you do, He will refresh you and provide the energy, strength, and wisdom you need for every situation.

Never ignore God's call to prayer. Many say they are too busy to stop and pray. Others seem afraid of what He may reveal to them if they do. They hesitate because they want to maintain control over their lives. This is foolish. Imagine trying to withhold something from the God of the universe—the One who knows all things, has created all things, and is over all things. All that sustains us in times of sin and resistance is the grace that He has extended to us. It is His grace that allows us to have a free will that is limited. In other words, God will let us go so far, but if we do not respond to His guidance, we will reap the consequences of our sinful action. He tells us in Numbers, "Be sure your sin will find you out" (32:23). Sin entails many decisions and actions. In every case, it leads to open rebellion against God.

Often the problems we face are the result of our decision to say no to God. He gave Adam and Eve a very straightforward command: "Don't eat the fruit of the tree in the center of the garden" (Gen. 2:16–17). Yet they ignored Him. They understood His command, yet they chose to disobey Him. Actually, they did not understand what the consequences of their sin would be. But God knew, and this is why we should obey Him—on the basis of who is doing the talking. If He says no or wait, we need to remember He knows much more than we know. He may be saving us from deep heartache. Or He could be in the process of preparing a great blessing for us to enjoy. If we rush ahead, we could end up in trouble or missing the very opportunity that will open a door of personal joy and satisfaction.

Another point you need to remember is this: you don't have to understand how God will solve your problems. He knows exactly what needs to be done. Your job is to set the focus of your heart on obeying Him. This includes seeking Him in prayer. If you are going to find a solution for your problems, you need to make this a top priority. Often the reason we do not receive answers to our prayers is because we are in a hurry. We are not willing to wait for God's answer. One of the most rewarding experiences you will have is watching God work as a result of waiting for His timing.

Timing is everything to God. He has an overarching plan for our lives and for the events of history. He knows when a small sparrow falls to the ground, and He knows when you need to take a step in a certain direction. The key to learning this principle is to be willing to wait for His timing, for His leading, and for His guidance. As you wait, set a goal to be in prayer. You can hold a prayer within your heart all day long or, for that matter, a week or even much longer. "God, heal my friend." "Save this person who does not know You." "Show me the way I need to go from this point forward." "Give me a promise to claim and to cling to when I sense the enemy drawing near with temptation." "Protect me." "Keep me focused on You so that I might know Your truth and hold it within my heart." There are countless prayers that you can pray in an instant and outside of the time that you spend in quiet devotion to Him. The king of Judah "turned his attention to seek the LORD" (2 Chron. 20:3). He did not call his commanding generals together. Instead, he went to the Lord in prayer, and God heard him. In fact, the Lord saw and heard the prayers of His people. Prayer should be a natural first response to any trouble you face.

Fear Not!

One woman confessed that she had become fearful over her situation. She also was dealing with a sense of dread concerning the future. Like the apostle Paul, she was dealing with a serious long-term illness that was painful and unrelenting. Pain can be a distraction or it can be a doorway of opportunity to know God better. The psalmist writes, "How blessed is the man whose strength is in You. . . . Passing through the valley of Baca they make it a spring" (Ps. 84:5–6). The word *Baca* means "weeping." In other words, the valley of Baca or the place of weeping becomes a spring of refreshment when God is the strength and the focus of our hearts. Whatever has your focus has you. If your mind is set on the Lord, then you will be able to walk through any valley knowing that He is right beside you. Fear has no power over you. It should be fleeting—a momentary emotion and not something we live with on a consistent basis. We have had friends say, "Oh, I wouldn't do that if I were you." Fear oozes from this type of comment. When we ask why, the answer is, "Something bad may happen." Thank goodness, Thomas Edison did not listen to the negative, defeating comments of his friends. Someone else would have discovered the lightbulb, or perhaps we would all still be using kerosene lamps.

When there is a true need for caution, God will provide it. He may ask you to do something that He would never require of another person. He may want to use you in some way that others do not understand. Once you have received His marching orders, there is only one thing to do, and that is to go forward by faith believing that even if the way before you seems closed, He will open it. If you never spend time with Him in prayer, you will not know what is best in times of trouble or even in the simple moments of life. You will be stagnant in your spiritual growth and flounder in your love for Him. Don't waste your sorrows. Ask Him to show you what He wants you to learn in difficult and foreboding circumstances.

The Power of Dependency

There are times when God will not allow you to solve a problem by yourself. He sends adversity, and He waits to see if you will call out to Him. Even though they had a large army,

Judah realized they could not win the battle. It was evident that they would lose. There will be times in our lives when we will know the same thing—that there is no way to win the confrontation apart from God's help. The truth is: God is never perplexed by your problems. Actually, He had the solution in mind before you were born and even before you knew there was a problem.

I can remember waking up one morning, and the first thing I was aware of was God's voice speaking to me. He said, "Today you need to seek wise, godly counsel." I began to pray, but the words came back to the forefront of my thinking, "You need to seek wise, godly counsel today." There was a pushing in my spirit that seemed to press against my heart. I knew that I needed to do exactly what He was telling me to do. One of the greatest assets you can have as a believer is a group of godly friends who love the Lord and are committed to living their lives for Him. Actually, you need at least one person who loves you no matter what and accepts you—just as you are. God is this type of friend to us, but He also desires for us to have friends whom we can turn to at times for confirmation and instruction.

There will be times when God uses a friend to help you solve the problem you are facing. Pride tells us that we do not need anyone else. We can be there for others, but we want to take care of personal matters without the help of anyone else. However, we cannot do it alone—we need one another. We need honest feedback at times, and we also need to know others are cheering for our success. When you select your closest friends, choose people who only want to grow in their walk swith the Lord and are committed to living godly lives. When you do, you will find that life is a lot smoother. Far too often, we draw close to people who have the ability to pull us down spiritually. Over the course of life, we will know all kinds of people. I'm talking about the ones who make up your inner circle of friends. Choose wisely, and you will find that you will be blessed beyond anything you can imagine by their fellowship. Once you learn how to be dependent on Him, God will usually allow you to be a part of the solution. But first, we must:

- focus,
- wait,
- listen, and
- obey.

Jehoshaphat and the people of Judah became very determined in their faith. There are times when you will need to remain perfectly still before God—times when the only thing you can do is trust Him—even though the situation may seem as though it is spinning out of control. The king continued his prayer, "Should evil come upon us, the sword, or judgment, or pestilence, or famine, we will stand before this house and before You (for Your name is in this house) and cry to You in our distress, and You will hear and deliver us" (2 Chron. 20:9). The entire nation had assembled before the Lord—

husbands and wives along with their children (v. 13). No one stayed home. The threat and the danger were far too real to ignore.

"Then in the midst of the assembly the Spirit of the LORD came upon Jahaziel the son of Zechariah . . . and he said, 'Listen, all Judah and the inhabitants of Jerusalem and King Jehoshaphat: thus says the LORD to you, 'Do not fear or be dismayed because of this great multitude, for the battle is not yours but God's" (vv. 14–15). We should want to shout, "Praise God," at the sight of these words. The Lord was about to show up on the scene in a mighty way.

When you earnestly seek Him, God will make you sensitive to His will. When He speaks to your heart, you will know it is His voice. Jesus underscores this point. In the book of John, He says, "My sheep hear My voice, and I know them, and they follow Me" (10:27). You may think, *God never speaks to me.* He speaks to those who have accepted Him as Savior, who have made Him Lord of their lives, and who take the time to listen. By listening, I mean being willing to be still before Him in prayer—still in your heart, mind, and spirit.

Prayer is a step of faith, not a pathway to anxiety. He calms our fears in His presence. We need to do what Jehoshaphat did and that was to convey his total dependence on God. I don't know the problem you are facing, but if you will write this down someplace where you can see it, God will draw your eyes back to these words: "Do not fear or be dismayed because of this great multitude, for the battle is not yours but God's." Here is the secret to victory: *God never loses.* He may not act as quickly as you want Him to act, but He is always perfectly on time—never late and never early.

Prayer Changes the Way We View Our Problems

One of the things that I think is easy to discern from this chapter is that God uses prayer to position us for victory. Prayer is something that we do as evidence of our love and worship of the Lord, but it also is a place of extreme security and empowerment. Some of the problems we face can only be solved on our knees. After the nation of Judah concluded their prayers to God, the Lord prepared them for battle, but He told them from the beginning that it was war, and they knew that they would not come away losers. The next morning, they marched into battle. However, a regiment of great warriors did not lead the way. Instead, the choir received the first-place nod from God. They were instructed to sing, "Give thanks to the Lord, for His lovingkindness is everlasting." The Bible tells us that when the people began singing and praising, the Lord set ambushes against the sons of Ammon, Moab and Mount Seir, who had come against Judah; so they were routed. "For the sons of Ammon and Moab, rose up against the inhabitants of Mount Seir destroying them completely; and when they had finished with the inhabitants of Seir, they helped to destroy one another. When Judah came to the lookout of the wilderness, they looked toward the multitude, and behold, they were corpses lying on the ground, and no one had escaped" (2 Chron. 20:22–24). God took care of the entire problem. Judah did not have to lift one bow or fire one arrow. The question that begs to be asked and answered is this: Where was the battle fought and won? There was only one place: on their knees. Had the king decided that the nation would not seek God's face but instead marched off to battle their enemies, the outcome would have been very different. With this in mind, how should we face our problems?

In Confidence

When you obey God, set your heart on Him, and commit your way to Him, He will take care of you. You do not have to be afraid because the problem facing you belongs to the Lord. It is not yours to bear alone. The moment the people of Judah realized this, they had no problem gathering a group of choir members to lead them into battle. In fact, being a member of that choir—singing praises to God—was probably the most exciting thing they had ever done. When you come to a point where you realize God's power lives within you and He is willing to fight every battle for you, then your confidence will be unshakable. You will be able to say with the psalmist, "For You are my hope; O Lord GOD, You are my confidence from my youth. . . . But as for me, I will hope continually, and will praise You yet more and more" (Ps. 71:5, 14).

On Our Knees

We pray knowing that He hears every word. "Therefore [Jesus Christ] is able also to save forever those who draw near to God through Him, since He always lives to make intercession for them" (Heb. 7:25). Once you have learned to trust God in prayer, the next step is to shift your prayers from being problem-centered to God-centered. Jehoshaphat did not begin his prayer with words of fear; he prayed with words of faith, exalting the Lord, praising Him, and also reminding Him of His faithfulness. Why do we "remind" God of the ways He has worked in our lives in the past? The main reason is to reset our minds from negative programming to confident, God-centered thinking. This is why it is crucial for us to pray, and read and study God's Word daily. The more we understand His ways, the greater our level of trust in Him.

In Obedience to God

When God tells you to do something, either you do it or you fail to gain His wisdom. Obedience is very important to the Lord. If God gives you a solution, are you willing to follow it? Are you willing to obey Him no matter what He requires? Sometimes there are risks involved. Sometimes the path He asks you to travel may seem very difficult and even unreasonable. It will demand faith and discipline on your part. But you will never regret obeying God. It is the only pathway to blessing and peace.

With the Right Mind-set

The prophet Isaiah writes, "For the LORD GOD helps Me, therefore, I am not disgraced; therefore, I have set My face like flint, and I know that I will not be ashamed" (Isa. 50:7). The author of Hebrews writes, "Let us run with endurance the race that is set before us, fixing our eyes on Jesus, the author and perfecter of [our] faith" (12:1–2). Set the focus of your heart on God. The reason is very simple. Satan will try his best to throw you off course. He will place one harmful distraction after another in front of you with the hope of discouraging you and convincing you to quit. Negative and fear-filled words, even when spoken by those we trust, can create an atmosphere of hesitation within our hearts. Instead of moving forward by faith, we will languish behind in feelings of doubt. Ask God to make you sensitive to the enemy's tactics, and keep your eyes set on Christ by studying His Word and applying His principles to your heart.

In Humility

Humility is a sign of submission. When we humble ourselves before the Lord, we reaffirm our faith in Him and our desire to do His will, regardless of the cost. We also confess that we want to lay down any sense of pride that we might have. Instead, we choose to obey Him, and this choice keeps us focused in the right direction. Pride leads to ruin, while humility leads to success and victory. The author of 2 Chronicles admonishes, "Put your trust in the LORD your

God and you will be established" (20:20). There should be no question in your mind. While you face trouble or sorrow, God is on your side. He wants to ease your burden. Struggling, apart from Him, against the weight of your fear only leads to exhaustion. "Therefore humble yourselves under the mighty hand of God, that He may exalt you at the proper time, casting all your anxiety on Him, because He cares for you" (1 Pet. 5:6–7).

With Expectation

King Jehoshaphat prayed, and then he waited for God's response. He was so sure that God would hear the voices of the people in prayer that the king called everyone together, and they stood before the Lord. Are you standing before the Lord with an expectant heart? I tell my congregation that we need to be on our knees before God in prayer. There is something about this position that demonstrates humility. Better yet, at times, bow down before Him in worship. When you do this, you will sense a strength rising up from within you that causes your spirit to stand and lift its face toward heaven in prayerful, hopeful expectation. The way you pray through a problem is by magnifying the power of God—focusing on His greatness and reminding Him of the promises He has given you. He will never fail you at any point in time. Trust, and you will see Him work mightily on your behalf.

CHAPTER 8

Lessons Learned from a Rebel

God instructed Jonah to head east to Nineveh, but he headed west across the Mediterranean Sea toward Tarshish and straight into trouble. Many of us have done the same thing. God makes it clear that He wants us to go in a certain direction, and we take another route! Imagine disobeying God. Yet each one of us has done this at some point. When we do, we miss a tremendous blessing and end up in desperate circumstances. In fact, most of the problems we face come as a direct result of not obeying the Lord. God tells us to go east, and we turn and go west.

When We Say No

Jonah was commissioned by God to take His word of salvation to the city of Nineveh. However, he refused to do this because the people living in that city were dire enemies of the Jewish people. Jonah did not want God to save the city; he wanted the Lord to destroy it and all who lived within its walls. Perhaps you have had a certain mind-set about something that God wants you to do. He may want you to say yes to a certain job, build a relationship with a neighbor, or take a position at your work that seems less than attractive. Maybe He wants you to take a certain path because He plans to use you in the lives of a group of people, but you are fighting hard against Him. When God tells us to take a step in a certain direction, we always need to obey Him. He knows what He wants to accomplish in our lives. He uses the forces of adversity and the power of unrelenting problems to:

- train us to do His will,
- refocus our lives so our hearts are set on Him, and
- prepare us for tremendous blessing.

Turning Our Attention Back to God

Walking away from God was not as easy as Jonah thought it would be. "The LORD hurled a great wind on the sea and there was a great storm on the sea so that the ship was about to break up. Then the sailors became afraid and every man cried to his god, and they threw the cargo, which was in the ship, into the sea to lighten it for them. But Jonah had gone below into the hold of the ship, lain down and fallen sound asleep" (Jon. 1:4–5).

There are times when God has to get our attention, and

many times He uses trials, difficulties, and disappointments to accomplish this. Jonah really had no intention of obeying God. In fact, once the winds picked up and the storm clouds gathered, he headed inside and down into the bottom of the ship so he did not have to witness what was taking place on deck. When the captain realized that the prophet was hiding out below, he wondered how a man of God could simply walk away knowing that danger was right before them (Jon. 1:6). Meanwhile, the crew was up on deck casting lots to see who was the one responsible for the horrendous storm, and "the lot fell on Jonah" (v. 7). Most of us know the rest of the story. Jonah surfaced and seeing what was taking place, knew that his days of running away from God were over. The Lord allowed adversity to strike to get his attention. God always knows exactly what to do to get our focus on His will. Jonah instructed the men to throw him overboard and into the raging sea. When they did, the waters immediately grew calm. God had Jonah right where He wanted him—in a position of humble surrender.

The Lord sent a large fish or whale to swallow His prophet and then to carry him back to land. Jonah had plenty of time (three days) to think about his life and role as God's prophet. From the belly of the whale he prayed,

> I called out of my distress to the LORD, and He answered me. I cried for help from the depth of Sheol; You heard my voice. For You had cast me into the deep, into the heart of the seas, and

the current engulfed me. All Your breakers and billows passed over me. So I said, 'I have been expelled from Your sight. Nevertheless I will look again toward Your holy temple.' . . .

You have brought up my life from the pit, O LORD my God. While I was fainting away, I remembered the LORD, and my prayer came to You, into Your holy temple. Those who regard vain idols forsake their faithfulness, but I will sacrifice to You with the voice of thanksgiving that which I have vowed I will pay. Salvation is from the LORD. (Jon. 2:2–4, 6–9)

When Jonah surrendered to God's will and admitted his failure to obey the Lord, God commanded the whale to deposit him on dry land in the direction of Nineveh. Then we read, "The word of the LORD came to Jonah the second time, saying, 'Arise, go to Nineveh . . . and proclaim to it the proclamation which I am going to tell you'" (Jon. 3:1–2). This time, Jonah obeyed God by preaching His Word to the people living in the city of Nineveh. They heard God's truth and turned away from evil.

Getting Back on Track

In his rebellion, Jonah realized that God was serious. He had chosen him for a particular task, and to continue to say no would be a deadly decision. Many times, God does not actually take our lives, but He certainly knows how to set us aside for a season of time until we are ready to listen and obey.

Most of us know when we are doing the opposite of God's will. We feel uncomfortable and restless. We may not sleep well, or we watch as our finances dwindle. There are countless ways for God to get our attention, and each one has the ability to produce enough stress to bring us to a point where we are ready to do whatever He wants us to do. He may want to restore a relationship that has been severed, or lead us to a place where we can finally sense His peace overflowing in our lives. He allows the winds of adversity to blow until we are knocked down and He has our attention. It is at this point—the point of surrender—when we begin to advance through the problem or difficulty.

One of the ways God solves our problems is by teaching us to listen for His corrective voice pointing out where we have taken a wrong turn. In Psalm 25, we discover that David is under extreme pressure. He had sinned against God, and guilt was eating him alive. He longed to experience the Lord's forgiveness and restoration.

> To You, O Lord, I lift up my soul. O my God, in You I trust, do not let me be ashamed; do not let my enemies exult over me. . . . Make me know Your ways, O Lord; teach me Your paths. Lead me in Your truth and teach me, for You are the God of my salvation. . . . Do not remember the sins of my youth or my transgressions; according to Your lovingkindness remember me, for Your goodness' sake, O Lord. (vv. 1–2, 4–5, 7)

All adversity, every problem you face, is a gift of love given to you from the hand of God. Whether you have followed the way of Jonah or not, adversity trains you to worship God and to long for time alone in His presence. He has three main purposes for allowing trouble and disappointment in our lives.

To Conform Us

This is God's ultimate purpose for allowing us to experience adversity. When the eyes of our hearts are set on doing only what we want to do, then we will not be able to hear God. Remember, Jesus took time to be alone with the Father. He did not do this to impress the disciples; He did it because He wanted to be just like His heavenly Father. The pressures of His world were just as great as they are in ours. Christ knew that to be like God, He had to spend time with Him. This is even truer for us. We may be saved by His grace, but we must conform to His image before we can reflect His love, grace, and mercy to others.

To Remind Us of His Great Love for Us

God loves us with an everlasting love. It is a love that is eternal and cannot be changed. God does not love us one day and then forget about us the next. He loves us when we are following Him and even when we get off course through sin and disobedience. Adversity is the tool He uses to guide us back to Him and to get our attention when we have gone our own way. Just as we discipline our children when they do wrong, God disciplines us.

To Provide an Opportunity for Self-Examination

The winds of adversity reveal the real person you are inside. When life is going well, you will never stop to think if there is anything wrong with what you are doing. Most people think that if life is going along smoothly, then God must be pleased with them. However, when the bottom drops out of life and problems begin to appear, we are much more likely to stop and pray, "Lord, show me if there is anything within me that is not pleasing to You." God allows the winds of adversity to blow long enough and strong enough until we are driven to examine what we are doing.

When you are being buffeted by adversity, one of the most natural things for you to do is to examine your heart to see if you are right before the Lord. "God, am I in Your will, or have I taken a step in the wrong direction? If the problem is not the result of sin, then are You trying to show me something?" God deals with root attitudes buried deep inside of us. Many of these have been in our lives since we were young. Those predetermined, preprogrammed attitudes often deal with our self-esteem and attitudes toward others. We may confess the problem and admit the sin, but this will not take care of it. God wants to change us so that our lives reflect His grace and mercy to others. He begins the process of sweeping our hearts clean.

If you respond to the situation and God the right way, He

will reveal where you have taken a wrong turn. Or if the problem has come as a natural result of life's sorrows and trials, He will give you the strength and wisdom you need to get through the difficulty. Regardless of the reason, the moment you cry out to God with an open and willing heart, He moves to comfort, encourage, and guide you. Remember, the intensity of His adversity is always limited to your capacity to bear it. He will never send adversity into your life and break your spirit. He will never use trouble or heartache to destroy you. He may use these to gain your love and attention, but in doing so, He always is working behind the scenes to build you up and bring you to a point where your life can be used for His maximum potential. Adversity is a tool God may use to shape your life. It can be a great source for spiritual growth or a point of discouragement. It all depends on how you allow Him to work in your life.

The key to overcoming problems is in our response to difficulties. God knows that heartache and disappointment are hard to bear. But He reminds us in Romans 8:28 that He would work all things together for our good and His glory. This means that even when we refuse to obey Him, once we have confessed our disobedience and asked Him to forgive us, He will do just that and also will restore our fellowship with Him.

If you are going through a dark time, when problems are stacked on every side, then you know that God is on the move in your life, and He has a great reward waiting for you when you yield your heart and life to Him.

CHAPTER 9

God's Purpose for Adversity

The young man was frustrated and watched closely for my response. Moments earlier, I had explained how God teaches us some of His greatest lessons in times of adversity. "But isn't there another way?" he asked. "Why does He allow us to hurt like I am hurting? I had no idea that I would lose my job and maybe my marriage, too. Will the pain that I feel inside ever stop?" I had heard these questions before from others.

Many times, we can identify with the hurt a person is feeling. However, there are other times when we simply cannot. We know what adversity feels like to us, but the problem in someone else's life may seem too great, the hurt too deep, and the sorrow too intense. Still, there is a common thread every problem we face: a desperate need to know that God understands and that He hears our prayers. We may not have a serious illness, but more than likely, we know what it feels like to face a difficulty that seems both overwhelming and debilitating. When you see someone who is hurting, ask God to give you the wisdom you need to respond with compassion and understanding.

In Psalm 18, the psalmist writes,

The Lord is my rock and my fortress and my deliverer, my God, my rock, in whom I take refuge; my shield and the horn of my salvation, my stronghold. I call upon the Lord, who is worthy to be praised. . . . In my distress I called upon the Lord, and cried to my God for help; He heard my voice out of His temple, and my cry for help before Him came into His ears. (vv. 2–3, 6)

God is our comforter in times of trial and sorrow. He is our refuge and strength when we feel as though we cannot face another trying day. He is our protection when problems grow too large for us to handle, and He is our shield and our deliverer. There is no reason for us to be fearful because He is with us at every moment and at every turn. He is sovereign. This means that He has full knowledge of the problem or sorrow that we are facing, and He is all-powerful—nothing is beyond His ability to heal or restore.

Believe in God's Ability

In Luke, we read how Jairus, an official of the synagogue, came to Jesus seeking healing for his twelve-year-old daughter. The Savior agreed to go with the man to his home to see the little girl. When Jesus and His disciples arrived at Jairus's house, they saw people weeping and overcome with sorrow.

Immediately, the Lord sought to assure them that the little girl was not dead. She was sleeping (Luke 8:52). Actually, the people had seen her die. From their viewpoint, there was no saving her. Earlier, Luke had recorded a conversation that Jesus had with Jewish officials who thought they had insight into God's way of thinking, but they did not. The Lord asked them, "Why are you reasoning in your hearts?" (Luke 5:22). Though the situation had changed, these people were doing the same thing. They were looking at their circumstances from a human perspective. The scribes and Pharisees had been concerned about sin, but these people were simply concerned that someone they loved deeply had died.

Jesus took the little girl by the hand and commanded her to sit up, "and her spirit returned, and she got up immediately" (Luke 8:55). Death is a part of life on earth. There are times when God intervenes, and those we love remain with us. However, there are other times when He allows our loved ones to go and be with Him. In each circumstance, we should ask Him to show us how to pray and then to give us the ability to see our situation from His perspective. These two steps of prayer based on Jeremiah 29:11 are essential to gaining His strength in times of adversity:

> Lord, show me how to pray so that I may know Your will for my life and my situation.
>
> Give me the ability to see my situation from Your perspective. Help me to understand that You have a future planned for me, and it is one full of hope and promise.

We may not fully understand the problems that we face, but God does perfectly. He knows the right words to speak to our hearts so that we are encouraged, lifted up, and sense His covering of protection falling down around us. However, we must be still enough in our spirits to hear Him when He speaks.

Are you listening? Or are you still talking nonstop to Him about the circumstances of your life? In times of crisis, He wants you to be still and know that He is God (Ps. 46:10). He has not forgotten you. In fact, He acknowledges the fact that your name is written on the very palm of His hand. "Can a mother forget the baby at her breast and have no compassion on the child she has borne? Though she may forget, I will not forget you! See, I have engraved you on the palms of my hands" (Isa. 49:15–16 NIV). With this truth in mind, why would you ever worry?

An Unplanned Storm

Adversity can be a swift teacher if you allow it to do its refining work in your life. We are never alone in our heartache. God is with us. At times, it may feel as though He is not listening or watching, but He is. He understands when we feel forgotten, weary, and overwhelmed. When the disciples were caught in a horrific storm on the Sea of Galilee, He was with them, but they did not know the extent of His care and love for them. Therefore, they cried out, "Teacher, do You not care that we are perishing?" (Mark 4:38). In their hearts, they knew Jesus did care, but they were afraid. More than likely, they did what many of us do. They waited to pray. The winds began to blow harder, and the waves grew higher, and still they tried not to cry out. But when it appeared that their boat would capsize and they would drown, they cried out to Him.

Jesus may have appeared to be sleeping, but He was completely aware of their circumstances, just as He is of yours. Have you ever wondered if Jesus is aware of your needs? He is, and He has a solution for the problems you face. In times of crisis, our goal should be to discover His will for our lives concerning the problem. Then we should ask Him to show us how we can faithfully obey Him. The fact is, in this particular situation, the Savior had been the One who instructed the disciples to leave the area where He had been teaching and row to the opposite side of the lake (Mark 4:35). There will be times in your life when God leads you out onto a stormy sea. From your perspective, it appears that you will drown. The sky is dark, the sea is swelling, and the wind is violent. You have no idea how you will survive, but God knows. He is the One who has led you to this point, and no matter how rough your sea becomes, He will carry you on to safety.

Don't overlook what Jesus told His disciples: He said, "Let us go over to the other side" (Mark 4:35). He said nothing about stopping midway and drowning. While He did not necessarily promise an easy, carefree journey, He certainly said nothing about dying or drowning. In fact, He said, "Let's go to the other side." In other words, they were going to make it, but no one in the group thought about the choice of Christ's words. How many of us stop along the way and become frightened by our circumstances? There are times when life becomes very difficult, and all we can do is believe in the One who has never failed us and keep moving forward until He tells us to stop.

A Matter of Focus

David writes, "The LORD is my shepherd, I shall not want. He makes me lie down in green pastures; He leads me beside quiet waters. He restores my soul; He guides me in the paths of righteousness for His name's sake. Even though I walk through the valley of the shadow of death, I fear no evil, for You are with me" (Ps. 23:1–4). Notice that David did not say, "If I get through the valley." He said, "Though I walk through." His focus was set on God—not on the shadows or the depth of his trouble but only on the Lord. Are you walking through a difficult time and wondering whether you will get through it or not? The answer always is yes when God is involved. The enemy may seek to tell you that you will not, but you will. Trust Him, obey Him, and then watch to see what He will do on your behalf. Adversity teaches us the importance of the following:

Obeying God

When my children were young, they would ask me what was the one thing they could learn about God's principles that would make a difference in their lives. I always told them to obey God, and leave all the details to Him. I am sure they have faced many trials, just as I have, but this one principle is foundational to every area of our Christian life. Obey God, and He will guide you *through* the stormy times to a place of great blessing. This may or may not mean material blessing. The true blessings of God can rarely be counted because He places them within our hearts. There is no eternal value that we can assign to the eternal love of God, the overflowing goodness of His mercy and grace, and His compassion that engulfs us and holds us secure and close whenever the winds of adversity blow hard against us. Obey God, and you will know what it means to walk in the light of His eternal love and grace.

David writes, "With your help I can advance against a troop; with my God I can scale a wall. As for God, his way is perfect; the word of the LORD is flawless. He is a shield for all who take refuge in him" (Ps. 18:29–30 NIV). A young woman who was struggling with a terminal illness ended up in my office insisting that she would visit her family over the Christmas holidays. She had been receiving treatment for several months, and her strength had faded. Still, she knew that one of the best medicines available to her was the love of her family and the presence of God in her life providing the support she needed. God is our very present help in times of trouble.

When Israel faced a serious threat from their enemies, Moses inquired of the Lord, saying, "If Your presence does not go with us, do not lead us up from here" (Ex. 33:15). Moses knew the value of having God lead the nation of Israel forward. In fact, he wanted to stay put if there was an outside chance that God was not going to go with them. Obedience teaches us to want the same thing. In other words, we want to be in God's will and not off on some trail that leads to serious trouble and disappointment.

If you are not sure about the direction you are about to take, pray as Moses prayed, "If Your presence does not go with me, then do not lead me up from here. Block my path, and guide me so that I will be in the center of Your will."

Listening for God's Direction

There is a mind-set in our world that tells us as long as we are doing good things, God will bless us. Satan loves to derail our lives by telling us that God really does not care where we end up. He wants us to think that the entire world is God's ministry, and whatever we choose to do is okay with Him. While not everyone is called into the ministry, each one of us certainly has been called by God to fulfill a certain purpose. There is no greater blessing than to know that you are doing what He has gifted you to do—whether it is on your job or in your church. Years ago, I preached a message entitled "Who's Doing the Talking?" In it, I demonstrated how we are constantly hearing different voices of reason—all of which, if we allow them, could drown out the voice of God. Remember, God spoke to Elijah through a whisper and not from the center of a raging storm. You may feel as though your life is in a vortex of trouble, but if you ask Him to show you how to be still before Him, He will; and in the calm of His presence, you will hear Him speak words of hope and encouragement. There are three ways God speaks to us today: through His Word, through His Holy Spirit who lives within the life of a believer, and through a trusted Christian friend or pastor. However, before you can hear His voice, you must be still enough to listen.

Living with a Sense of Perfect Peace

David learned to wait before the Lord, and we need to do the same. God's timing is perfect. He knows when to tell you to move forward. Until He does, you can rest knowing that the Prince of Peace is at work in your life. When trouble comes, we think, *I've got to do something.* An opportunity presents itself, and we jump at it. People sink deeper into debt because they refuse to be still and listen for God's guidance. They jump ahead of the Lord and then wonder why their lives are so troubled. Before they know it, they have added layer upon layer of problems that they cannot control. This can be true of someone who has lost a spouse or job. The death of a loved one is devastating. Being laid off from a job we like can strike hard against our self-esteem.

After the sudden death of his wife, a middle-aged man announced to his friends that he could not be alone. He needed a wife. Therefore, he remarried and quickly risked bypassing God's best to meet a need in his life. He did not even know if what he was doing was right. He just knew that he had a need and could not wait any longer. Loneliness is not something only single people face. It is something that comes from not being at peace in God's presence and not being satisfied with what He has provided. A person can be lonely even though in a room full of people. Never allow loneliness to drive you to do something that you will regret later. God has your need well within His sight, and He will meet it according to His timetable.

Who Can Identify with Your Sorrows?

Jesus Christ died a cruel death so that you might have eternal life. He knows exactly the struggle you are facing. The Bible tells us, "For since He Himself was tempted in that which He has suffered, He is able to come to the aid of those who are tempted" (Heb. 2:18). He understands the temptations you face. He knows the frustration of your heart, the feelings of rejection that threaten to overwhelm you with sadness, and the burdens you bear that seek to crush every notion of hope within you.

In the Garden of Gethsemane, Christ prayed, "My Father, if it is possible, let this cup pass from Me; yet not as I will, but as You will" (Matt. 26:39). Just as we have done, Christ asked if there was another way for God to accomplish His will. No one, not even the Savior, enjoys the thought of adversity. However, no sooner had this thought passed over His lips than He professed His willingness to obey God: "Yet not as I will, but as You will." Surrender is not a symbol of weakness for the Christian. It is a demonstration of tremendous strength—the same strength that Paul talked about in Philippians 4:13 when he wrote, "I can do all things through Him who strengthens me." When life turns stormy and we cannot see the shoreline, we may not have the strength to trust God, but Christ within us will give us this ability.

When problems come, we also wonder if we have done something wrong. Are we out of step with God's plan? Is sin involved? While these are important questions, the greater question is, "Lord, how do You want me to respond to this problem?" If you have fallen into sin and are living apart from God's fellowship, then you know what you need to do—ask Him to forgive you and restore you spiritually so that you might enjoy His goodness again. If you have refused, like Jonah, to do what He has asked you, tell Him that you have been rebellious and that you want to get back on track with Him. God will not refuse you. In fact, He will embrace you with open arms.

The difficulty and trial that you are facing may simply be the result of God's desire to test your faith and strengthen you for a greater blessing. If you sense that this is the case, tell Him that you are willing to remain right where you are until He moves you forward. Always keep in mind that God uses the circumstances of life to conform us to His image. He strengthens our faith and tests our ability to trust Him by allowing difficulty at work and also in our relationships with others. Often, pride is hiding out just beneath the surface of our hearts, and God knows that when He turns up the pressure, it will be exposed and then He will deal with it. He always has a purpose for the trials He allows to touch our lives. The thorn in the apostle Paul's life was allowed by God to keep the apostle from being prideful. The difficulties that David faced were sent to prepare him to rule Israel. The suffering that New Testament believers faced was used to strengthen their faith and as a testimony to each of us.

Our response to every trial is crucial. We have the choice to become bitter or to grow stronger in our faith. Years ago, noted evangelist J. R. Miller wrote in *For the Best Things*:

Sometimes it is very dark. We cannot understand what we are doing. We do not see the web we are weaving. We are not able to discover any beauty, any possible good in our experience. Yet if we are faithful and fail not and faint not, we shall some day know that the most exquisite work of all our life was done in those days when it was so dark.

If you are in the deep shadows because of some strange, mysterious providence, do not be afraid. Simply go on in faith and love, never doubting. God is watching, and He will bring good and beauty out of all your pain and tears.

You may feel as though your life has been burned to the ground and nothing recognizable remains. However, God sees potential even when you are blinded to the hope your life contains. God promises us "[beauty or] a garland instead of ashes, the oil of gladness instead of mourning" (Isa. 61:3). For God's people, ashes are a sign of grief, unworthiness, humiliation, and penitence. They are also used as a symbol of deep humility and need. In his misery and sorrow, Job sat in ashes, but God restored all that he had lost to an even greater degree. He never subtracts; He always multiplies.

No one can escape adversity. Either we are passing through a dark valley or we see one approaching. Life is full of trials. However, it is brimming with victory, too. God uses difficulty to shape and mold us so that we become men and women of faith—people that reflect His love and mercy to others. Jesus knew the disciples could not minister to others until their lives had been broken by adversity. Each time the Savior allowed some hardship to come their way, He was preparing them for the future and for their ministry. We are trained by life's difficulties to either trust God or ourselves. If we trust the Lord, we will never know defeat. We may suffer at times, be disappointed, and even face discouragement, but we will never lack anything. God is faithful, and He will provide exactly what we need, when we need it.

CHAPTER 10

How to Find Clear Guidance

Have you ever needed to make a decision but had no idea what God wanted you to do? You wanted to do what was best, but you were not sure what that was. You were standing at a crossroads—a place where the road divides before you—and you wondered whether to turn right or left or stay where you were.

God always has a plan in mind. The challenge for most of us is how to discover it. Many people make a mistake by believing they cannot discern His will. They think it is either hidden or difficult to know, or that He makes His will known to others but not to them. This just is not true. He is willing to speak to each one of us, but we must be in a position where we can hear His voice. The nation of Israel spent forty years wandering in the wilderness as a result of *not* listening to God. He led the people to the very door of the promised land, but they refused to go in and claim what He had given them. They were frightened at the sight of their enemies, and they forgot who was leading them—the Lord of heaven and earth. Throughout the years that followed this moment of disobedience, God remained committed to Israel. No matter how many wrong turns they took, He was determined to teach them how to hear His voice and to do what He had given them to do, which was to enter a land of goodness and blessing. God is long-suffering. He will never give up on you. He sees all that lies behind you and knows all that is up ahead. He is omniscient and committed to your success because He knows that when you succeed, you bring honor and glory to Him.

One Decision After Another

Forty years after Israel had turned away from the land God had given to them, He brought them back to the same place. There are times in our own lives when we refuse to do what the Lord has asked us to do. We may have missed doing His will due to ignorance or disobedience. So often, problems that arise in our lives come as a result of our not obeying God. We may be focused only on our desires, but He coaches us to turn in another direction. Still, we ignore His voice, and as we said earlier, we suffer the consequences of our disobedience. This is exactly what the nation of Israel did. Forty years later, after wandering in the desert, God brought them back to the place where they had disobeyed Him. Essentially, He gave them another opportunity to obey and gain access to His blessing. This time, they obeyed and entered the land.

God's main form of communication is through His Word, but there are times when He speaks to us through the circumstances of life. The closer we are to Him, the greater our level of discernment will be. The first time Israel approached the land, they were only concerned about their needs. The second time, their focus had changed. Now, they were focused on doing what God wanted them to do. Isn't it amazing how adversity sharpens our outlook and helps us see the will of God for our lives?

Problems and trials will come, and we will wonder what He is doing. Difficulty, heartache, and disappointment are the very tools He uses to teach us to honor and trust Him in greater ways. We need His clear guidance so we can avoid the pitfalls of life, but we also need to learn to listen. Israel did not go into the land the first time because they were frightened. They did not even cross the boundary line because they were shaking with fear over the sight of their enemies. Israel forgot an important principle: when God calls you to do something, He provides all you need to accomplish the task. All you need to do is obey Him and go forward—without hesitation—by faith.

If you do not learn the lesson you need to learn the first time, God will do what He did with Israel—He will bring you back to the same point at another time to see if you are willing to obey Him. The next time Israel approached the promised land, they had a different perspective. They were ready to enter it. The years they had spent in the wilderness and the desert had helped to refocus their hearts on one thing: doing exactly what God wanted them to do. Regardless of the effort, they were committed, and you can learn to do the same thing. When you do, you will experience one victory after another. Your life will be framed in peace and a deep sense of joy. You also will have hope. Just as there are consequences to sin, there are consequences to obedience. One of these is hope—hope for the future, hope for the present, and hope in all that you do.

God Provides the Guidance You Need

You may be a person who is experiencing a change in your vocation or a financial crunch. Someone reading this could be in the process of making a decision about marriage. Or a couple may be praying about the college their son or daughter wants to attend. Each day, you make hundreds, if not thousands, of decisions. Your circumstances feel urgent. And for the believer who wants to walk in the power of God's Spirit, they are. Every decision is important to God. He wants to give you direction and guidance so you will not get off track or make a mistake. Far too often, we want to see miles beyond where we are standing. The reason living life for Christ is a walk of faith is because this is what we are called to do. Trust Him for today and tomorrow and all the days that will follow. Remember, He went out before the nation of Israel, and He will do the same for you.

When Moses turned to face the burning bush, God began to instruct Him. Immediately, the Lord provided direction: "I am the God of your father, the God of Abraham, the God of Isaac, and the God of Jacob.' . . . I have surely seen the affliction of My people who are in Egypt, and have given heed to their cry because of their taskmasters, for I am aware of their sufferings. So I have come down to deliver them. . . . I will send you to Pharaoh, so that you may bring My people, the sons of Israel, out of Egypt'" (Ex. 3:6–8, 10). He also gave Gideon the insight he needed at just the right point in time (Judg. 7). He did the same for the apostle Paul. In Acts 16, he was headed in a certain direction to preach the gospel when God's Spirit spoke to him, stopping him from going forward.

> They passed through the Phrygian and Galatian region, having been forbidden by the Holy Spirit to speak the word in Asia; and after they came to Mysia, they were trying to go into Bithynia, and the Spirit of Jesus did not permit them; and passing by Mysia, they came down to Troas.
>
> A vision appeared to Paul in the night: a man of Macedonia was standing and appealing to him, and saying, "Come over to Macedonia and help us." When he had seen the vision, immediately we sought to go into Macedonia, concluding that God had called us to preach the gospel to them. (Acts 16:6–10)

Was God uninterested in the cities of Asia Minor? Certainly not! He just had a different plan in mind. He knew the direction He wanted the apostle to go. Therefore, His

Spirit redirected the team of missionaries. Later, Paul would travel through this region preaching God's truth and seeing many people come to Christ. However, this moment was not the time for that. Remember, timing is everything to God. He knows exactly when to motivate us to move forward and when to hold us back. God has not stopped talking. He continues to speak to those who have accepted His Son as their Savior. However, to hear His voice, we must surrender our wills to Him and be willing to wait—if necessary, indefinitely—until He leads us to the next step. Waiting is an active step of faith and obedience. Paul obeyed the Lord and his ministry stayed right in step with God's plan.

God Wants to Speak to You

He is just as interested in speaking to you as He was to Moses, Paul, Daniel, Peter, David, John, and so many more. In Psalm 32:8, the Lord says, "I will instruct you and teach you in the way which you should go; I will counsel you with My eye upon you." This is a clear promise from the Lord that He will give you direction for your life. In Proverbs, He tells us, "Trust in the LORD with all your heart and do not lean on your own understanding. In all your ways acknowledge Him, and He will make your paths straight" (3:5–6). These verses provide specific promises telling us that God will guide and instruct us. We do not have to leave home or even pick up the telephone to call a friend to gain eternal wisdom about our lives and any problem we may have.

He is our instructor, guide, and teacher. But sometimes we do not hear what He is saying because we are too wrapped up in our problems. We pray and think we are giving our burden to Him, but we continue to carry it around by talking about it and even frantically wondering what will happen next. When we ask God to take our burdens, He does. However, if we continue to cling to it and work on ways of solving it, we signal a lack of faith in His ability.

Our Burden-Bearer

When faced with a difficult problem, you can respond three different ways:

You can continue to struggle with it and bear the weight of the situation alone. Many people who do this end up suffering emotionally and physically. They become weary and discouraged, which plays right into Satan's hand. God did not create us to carry huge emotional burdens. He wants to be our burden-bearer, but we must submit control of the situation and our lives to Him.

I have watched as people have hung on to their problems believing if they just worked hard enough, they could come up with a solution. Even if we could, do we only want the solution that we can achieve? Or do we want what God provides? Often, the enemy whispers, "You need to stay in control to get what you want." The truth is, we only need to do what God is requiring us to do. When rolling our burdens over onto Him, He will provide the answer we need along with the peace and release our hearts long to experience. We can be worried, or we can be discerning and give God the opportunity to work infinitely on our behalf.

You can run from it and avoid dealing with it. Many people have an "I'll deal with it tomorrow" attitude, or "I'll pretend the problem is not there, and it will go away" mindset. Problems don't just go away. They need to be solved, and you can either ask God to give you wisdom to know how to handle it or you can wait, deny it is there, and watch your stress level grow to a point where it is unbearable.

You can surrender the problem and yourself to God's care. For the believer, this is the only real solution. God is concerned about every area of your life. He never sees your burden as being insignificant. He knows small issues can quickly develop into large problems. Therefore, no matter how large or small a difficulty may appear, make a habit of praying about it. Through the difficulties of life, God is training you to come to Him in times of trouble and in times of joy and gladness. He never wants you to view your time in prayer as just a place to dump your worries. He has a greater purpose in mind. He wants you to develop a desire to know Him intimately. Instead of going to God in prayer with a list of things you think you need, spend time with Him in worship. Praise Him and tell Him that you only want to live your life for Him. Rest in His presence, and you will find that He knows exactly what you need even though it was never mentioned. When you face a difficulty, God wants you to do the following:

- Seek Him in worship and prayer.
- Declare your faith in Him.
- Be willing to wait, if necessary for His solution.
- Learn to rest in His presence, knowing that He is working behind the scenes on your behalf.
- Move forward when He directs you without questioning His method or motive.
- Claim the victory, because regardless of the outcome, God has promised to work all things together for our good and His glory (Rom. 8:28).

Sometimes, the only evidence you or I have in addressing a problem is the guidance of the Holy Spirit who continues to impress upon us to move in a certain direction of faith. If we only make decisions based on what we can see or the information we have at the moment, we will miss a tremendous blessing. God has an infinite information service. He knows all there is to know about everything we are facing and how the outcome will affect our lives later. It is shocking how many people waste money trying to find out something about their future. They risk entanglement with a side of the spiritual realm that God does not want them to encounter. Believers should never consult anyone about the future other than God. He is the only One who knows the absolute truth. Horoscopes are strictly the enticement of the enemy to lure you away from the Word of God. We need to avoid this and anything else that would deny God's power in favor of spiritualism and worldly reasoning.

There are six elements that are essential to helping you find God's solution for the problems you face.

Pathway

To discover God's will for your situation, you must realize that He has a step-by-step plan for you to follow. The first step includes confession of sin. There are people who believe that they can say a quick prayer and God will answer it without requiring anything from them. However, they overlook the fact that God's first desire is for us to draw near to Him in order to enjoy His presence and fellowship. We worship Him first. Like Moses, we come to Him, bow down, and remove our "sandals" as a symbol that we know we are on holy ground (Ex. 3:5).

Second, lay down your personal desires. This is essential to overcoming the difficulties of life. Sometimes God allows hardship to coach us into giving Him full control of our lives. Years ago, a young girl struggled for some time to tie her shoes. She did not want her father to help her. He allowed the battle to go on. Finally, standing outside her bedroom door, he heard his young daughter say, "God, I just can't do it. Please help me." God is waiting for us to say, "I just can't do this. I need your help." As long as we are pressing to reach our desires without considering what the Lord wants us to do, we will run into conflict. You can tell the Lord, "Father, this is what I truly want to do. I place my desires in neutral. Please show me Your will for my situation so I can be obedient to You."

Patience

A sign of genuine maturity is patience. James writes, "Let endurance have its perfect result, so that you may be perfect and complete, lacking in nothing" (James 1:4). In other words, let patience complete its work in your life so that you will be mature, wanting nothing other than what God in His grace and mercy gives freely to you. Have you ever considered the gifts that God gives? Many times, people avoid praying about a problem because they do not want to face it for fear that God will punish them or withhold His goodness. God gives good gifts to His children. He wants us to be so in tune with Him that we find all our needs met in Him. He not only provides answers to problematic situations, He also provides the very things we long to receive—friendships, gifts, and even possessions for our enjoyment—as long as our first and only goal is to live our lives for Him.

Remember His promise to us in Psalm 84, "The LORD God is a sun and shield . . . no good thing does He withhold from those who walk uprightly" (v. 11). And James reminds us, "Every good thing given and every perfect gift is from above, coming down from the Father of lights, with whom there is no variation or shifting shadow" (1:17). It is very important that you are patient with the Lord, because patience indicates that you are willing to be emptied of selfish activity and to have victory over the urge to make a snap decision. It also means you want to wait on God's timing instead of rushing to take action when what you are doing may not be His best. Never rush to make a decision. Instead, wait until you have God's mind concerning the problem or the circumstance you are facing. If you will do this, then you will gain tremendous insight into God's character, attributes, and personal love for you.

Pressure

When it comes to making right decisions, I believe this is the greatest enemy we face. There are two types of pressure:

External: This is the pressure that comes from the opinions of others. I call it "people pressure." It often involves the pressure of time. For example, someone will say, "You have to make a decision in three days." This type of demand can set the stage for extreme pressure. You feel pressured to make a decision now rather than later. There are some major decisions in life where we need to take time—days, weeks, or even months—to understand God's will and mind. There are other times when we need to move forward by deciding what needs to be done. The Lord understands time restraints. He knows when you truly do need to make a decision, and will make His will known in accordance with the need you have. Therefore, never allow yourself to be pressured by others if you know that God is prompting you to wait. On the other hand, do not allow the enemy to hold you back from stepping forward to make a decision that is clearly God's best for you.

Internal: This comes when the Holy Spirit is coaching us to make a decision or to deal with a situation. Pressure in this way means we do not really have clear guidance and direction for a decision that we are considering. It is God's way of saying, "Be patient. Don't yield to the pressure of those externally who would force you to make a decision when you are not ready." You may not have all the facts. Therefore, when the pressure increases, tell the Lord, "I'm Your servant. It is my duty [you are duty-bound to be obedient to God] to obey You. In order for me to do this, I need to know Your will for my situation. I cannot follow unless You are guiding me. Please open my heart and mind to Your plan and show me exactly what You want me to do. So, Lord, I'm waiting patiently for You, refusing to be pressured into anything. I have cleared my mind and my heart of any known sin or personal desire. Now, Lord, tell me what You want me to do."

Prayer

Often, when it comes to prayer, the key to hearing God's voice and gaining His wisdom is learning to persist in prayer. You may think that prayer is something that you do only in the morning during your quiet time with God or late in the evening after the children are asleep. However, prayer is a lifestyle. And we can live in a state of prayer even when we are going about our normal routines. Learning to pray God's way includes persistence, waiting, and listening. Through prayer, He prepares us for His answer. He points out the areas that need to be addressed, but He also teaches us His principles to live by. There will be times when God withholds an answer until we have submitted to His will. Ultimately, prayer is a method He uses to position us for blessing.

Promise

The same God who led Abraham away from his home in Ur is willing to lead you through the difficulty you are facing. And the same Lord who led the nation of Israel into the promised land desires to do the same for you—to lead you to a place of extreme blessing and hope. He wants to guide you—to give you wisdom and to provide for every need you have. It begins with a promise: "Call to Me and I will answer you, and I will tell you great and mighty things, which you do not know" (Jer. 33:3).

There are countless promises in God's Word. Begin to read it with an open and submitted heart, and you will discover fresh hope and enough courage to face each day. The psalmist writes, "I will hear what God the LORD will say; for He will speak peace to His people, to His godly ones" (Ps. 85:8). Here also is a warning about opening the Bible and looking for an answer without truly seeking God. People also have told me that they just opened God's Word and found a scripture that seemed to justify their actions.

Sometimes they were sinful actions. You never want to flip open the Bible and scan the text for an answer or for justification for what you want to do. This is highly dangerous, but you definitely want to study His Word and over time, you will gain insight into God's solution for your problems. When you spend time with Him, He reveals Himself to you.

Peace

In Colossians 3:15, God gives us a beautiful promise that we can claim for our lives and the difficulties we face: "Let the peace of Christ rule in your hearts." Paul is saying that we need to learn how to let peace be an umpire over our hearts. When the peace of God is standing sentinel over your heart, fear, anxiety, depression, and anger will not be able to set up a stronghold.

A sense of perfect peace is evidence that you are either in the middle of God's will or that you have made the necessary adjustment to get to that point.

Having God's peace comes as the result of having the right focus. When your heart and mind are set on Christ, you will not be shaken, even when the winds of adversity kick up around you or the threat of failure comes swiftly like a flood. Peace—God's peace—will rule your heart. If someone is seeking to push you into making a decision, refuse to budge until you know that you have a sense of peace from God.

The final confirmation that you have God's peace is a

sense of rest within your life. You are not rushing to meet life head-on. Instead, you are operating alongside God with a supernatural strength and sense of discernment that come from surrendering your life to Him. The struggle to do more, get ahead, experience more, and gain more has ended. You have a sense of peace, not because of what you have, but because of who has you, and this is your greatest reward—life everlasting lived out in the arms of unconditional love and infinite grace!

The Mighty Hand of the Lord

When the nation of Israel reached the promised land, God instructed them to collect twelve stones from the Jordan River from the place where the priests had been standing (Josh. 4). These stones represented the twelve tribes of Israel. God had delivered the nation into the land, and now they were about to build a memorial to Him—one that would be a reminder of His faithfulness to future generations. Joshua said to the people,

> When your children ask their fathers in time to come, saying, "What are these stones?" then you shall inform your children, saying, "Israel crossed this Jordan on dry ground."
>
> For the LORD your God dried up the waters of the Jordan before you until you had crossed, just as the LORD your God had done to the Red Sea, which He dried up before us until we had crossed; that all the peoples of the

earth may know that the hand of the LORD is mighty, so that you may fear the LORD your God forever. (Josh. 4:21–24)

Have you set up a memorial to God for the times He has delivered you from your enemies? Maybe you keep a daily journal and can look back to see the many ways He has worked in your life. Regardless of how you do it, He wants you to recall His faithfulness and live with the promise that no matter how great a trial appears, He will help you solve it.

CHAPTER 11

Reaching Your Full Potential

Some of the most painful and difficult times of my life have been when God was in the process of breaking me to prepare me for greater service. I have never enjoyed this process, although I know the outcome always leads to growth and blessing. Most people feel the same way. There is enough independence left within us that we want to draw back and avoid anything that resembles hardship or trouble. Yet these are the very tools God uses to increase our faith and prepare us for the next step. The message of brokenness does not appeal to those who only want to live for themselves and not for God. While none of us would be eager to sign up to experience a season of brokenness, we can learn to endure it with patience and steadfast hope once we understand that God sees our potential and has a plan for the adversity He allows to touch our lives.

For Those Who Bear Heavy Burdens

Throughout this book, we have discussed King David and others whom God has used. One of the primary characteristics of David's life was that he had a heart for God (Acts 13:22). However, if you did not know anything about his life other than the years he spent running away from King Saul and the threat of death, you would be tempted to wonder what God was doing.

In 1 Samuel 16, the Lord instructs the prophet Samuel to anoint David king of Israel, but nothing significant happened in this direction for a long time. Imagine being called into the office of the CEO of your company and being told that you had just received a very important promotion. In your mind, it is time to clean out the desk in the cubicle you have been working in for the past three years and get ready for a move to an upstairs office with windows and a pastoral view of woodlands. But nothing happens. You pray, and God confirms that He has a plan for your life and especially for your circumstances.

David may have had times of disillusionment, but we never read of him wanting to do anything other than to achieve the goal that God had set for him. If that meant waiting, then he was ready to wait indefinitely. His relationship with the Lord was tightly woven with threads of faith, hope, love, and surrender. You will never reach your full potential as long as you look at your circumstances and say, "God, I can't," or "God, I won't." The truth is: brokenness is a pathway to blessing. But it also is the way God uncovers our true potential. Rarely does He use people until He has broken them. This process can be very painful, but one of the best ways to advance through it is to surrender your problems and fears to the Lord. Be willing to obey Him, and be willing to wait or move forward at His command.

Clinging to disappointments and feelings of anger and frustration only prolong the journey. These also have the potential to tempt us to doubt God's goodness and plan. Resist feelings of self-pity, especially when the enemy whispers, "This is the end," "You will never get out from under this burden," or "You are alone, and there is no one to help you." Friends and family members can be great encouragers, but they also can be tempted to offer discouragement instead of faithful support. Remember what Job's wife suggested when he faced severe temptation? She told him, "Do you still hold fast your integrity? Curse God and die!" (Job 2:9). He ignored her negative counsel and said, "Though He slay me, I will hope in Him" (13:15).

Know When to Let Go

Have you ever felt like Moses, David, or Job? You have come to a point in your life where you want to say, "Lord, this problem is too great for me—too vast, too heavy, and too hurtful. I can't handle it alone." This was where Moses found himself—wondering how he would continue at such a stiff pace with such an unwilling group of people. Numbers 11 outlines the nation of Israel's decline in the area of morale. With the excitement of their escape from Egypt behind them, they began to think about what they had done and the inconveniences of living on the road. This is when they began to complain and murmur against Moses and the Lord. God was not pleased with their actions or words. He had provided their freedom from slavery, but they wanted even more. Even more devastating, they really did not want anyone to tell them what they could or could not do.

Moses became so depressed by the actions of the people that he actually told the Lord, "If You are going to deal thus with me, please kill me at once, if I have found favor in Your sight, and do not let me see my wretchedness" (Num. 11:15). The bottom line is, Moses wanted to die! And he needed to let go and allow God to take control of his life and circumstances. There will be times in each one of our lives when God gives us a task to do that appears far too great for us to handle. At first, prideful thoughts can tempt us to think we can handle the job no matter how great the challenge may seem. However, God did not create us to work independently of Him. We can do nothing apart from Him.

If you want to reach your full potential, allow God to

have the problems that you are facing. Surrender them to Him. It may seem simple when written in black and white, but it is rare. Many people believe they have given their problems to God, but they have not. They lay them down only to pick them up again. How do you know when you are still carrying a burden or a problem? Usually, you know by the weight of the burden. If it is heavy to the point of being destructive, you must stop and ask God to show you if He wants you to bear this load on your own. Earlier, we mentioned how Jesus instructed His followers with these words, "Come to Me, all who are weary and heavy-laden, and I will give you rest. Take My yoke upon you and learn from Me, for I am gentle and humble in heart, and you will find rest for your souls. For My yoke is easy and My burden is light" (Matt. 11:28–30).

The Savior wanted the people to give their burdens to Him. In New Testament times, a yoke was used to couple animals together so they could work more effectively. Jesus used this term with a positive application. He is teaching us that His yoke is easy, light, and much more productive. When we share our burdens with Him, He comes alongside us and lifts the yoke up so that it is not weighing us down. But if we insist on shouldering the weight alone, we will fall and not get up. Everything boils down to a matter of trust. Do you trust God with your problem, your future, and your immediate circumstances?

His Eye Is Set on the Goal

God always has His eye set on the finish line. But He also is very concerned about how we arrive at the point of destination. Israel came to the doorway of the promised land but refused to enter because they believed they knew better than the Lord. They had not learned what it meant to submit to His will and plan for their lives. However, forty years later, the attitude of the nation had changed. Instead of resisting His will, they knew to obey and entered the land without hesitation. God had trained them through the difficulties they had faced. Therefore, the time they had been in the wilderness was not wasted. God had prepared them to receive the promise and the blessing He had given years earlier.

In times of training and brokenness, God targets specific areas in our lives that are hindering His purpose and will. He arranges the circumstances for our brokenness and also chooses the tools by which this will be accomplished. He also controls the emotional and physical pressure that is applied to our life. All of this is done in an effort to teach us how to submit to His will. God created us for Himself and for His purposes. Paul writes, "Do you not know that your body is a temple of the Holy Spirit who is in you, whom you have from God, and that you are not your own? For you have been bought with a price: therefore glorify God in your body" (1 Cor. 6:19–20).

The people who have the greatest difficulty with submission to God usually are the ones who have no desire to live their lives solely for Him. They would rather go to church on Sunday, but leave God out of the rest of their week. When they do, they miss the greatest source of blessing and hope known to man, which is an intimate relationship with the Savior—the God of the universe who loves them unconditionally. By saying no to God, they never fully experience the dynamic presence of His Spirit living in them. The source of our strength shifts from our limited ability to His infinite resources. We may feel the pressure as it rises, but we also have clarity and can make right choices as we roll the problem over onto the Lord. We allow Him to give us the wisdom we need to solve it without having to carry a mental and physical weight that is far too great for us to bear. God has a purpose and a plan for every situation we face. In fact, you cannot think of a problem that is too great or vast for Him.

One of the reasons brokenness is such a painful experience is because God works at deep levels. He also deals with the very issues that we do not want Him to touch. Ultimately, He wants to control every aspect of our lives. And the last thing we want to do is surrender this type of access to anyone—including the Lord. Earlier, we talked about the apostle Paul and how God allowed him to face tremendous suffering (2 Cor. 12:7). As we read his letters, and especially Acts, we find that Paul faced great opposition. However, he never lost sight of the goal that God had given him. And he stopped resisting God and opened himself up to the corrective hand of the Lord.

When problems come, our greatest challenge is to remember that He uses adversity to bring us to a point of surrender so we can reach our full potential. Once Paul accepted Christ, his life changed. His personal goals shifted and suddenly became very unimportant to him. The only thing that mattered was his service and dedication to the Lord. Brokenness brings clarity and focus to our lives. Paul may have struggled with many of the same temptations we face, but he was determined to continue to live for the truth he was called to proclaim (Rom. 7).

One of the most spiritually dangerous thoughts you can have is, *I'm glad I have learned that lesson.* As soon as we allow those words to pass through our minds, we should sense a check in our spirits. We never completely learn all there is to learn when it comes to areas such as pride, forgiveness, waiting on God, and much more. We may learn a great deal about these areas, but there is so much more that God wants to teach us. Paul was not an exception to this rule. Throughout his life, he faced one valley experience after another (2 Cor. 11 and 12). He was beaten on several occasions, shipwrecked at least twice, and was always under the threat of the Judaizers, who were eager to mount an opposition to his work. We might be tempted to wonder, *Why would God call a man like Paul into the ministry and then allow him to face severe suffering?*

There are several lessons in this area that God wants us to learn. They are the same ones that He wanted to teach Paul.

We cannot live the Christian life apart from God. When Paul came to know Christ, he quickly realized that God was his new instructor. The lessons he had learned as a Jewish scholar were no longer valid as solutions for the problems he faced. His new grid system was based on the saving grace and mercy of the Lord Jesus Christ. Everything changed in Paul's life. The knowledge he deemed as being so important suddenly appeared weak and invalid. Though I'm sure there were times when he wanted to rise up and say, "I know how to solve this situation. After all, I have a degree. I know the answer," he did not do it. He learned to listen for God's voice directing and guiding him through one difficulty after another.

How do you resist using the human knowledge and ability you have learned over the years?

Ask God to help you see your circumstances from His perspective. In the heat of the battle, when conflict arises, you must train yourself to stop and wait for God's guidance. This can take place in a matter of seconds. Or it can be something that transpires over time. Often, I'm asked, "What do I do in times of emergency?"

My answer is this: God knows the emergency is coming even before it appears. Let the first words you whisper in prayer to Him be words of humble submission. "Lord, I don't understand what is happening. Please show me what to do." The moment He hears this type of prayer, He will be moved.

He may open a door of escape, or He may be quiet and want you to wait. I imagine that after His conversion to Christ, Paul wanted to tell everyone about what had happened to him, especially those in Jerusalem. However, notice that he did not do this. Instead, he went away into Arabia where he spent time alone with God in His classroom—studying at His feet. Most people want to rush into action. They want to solve the problem, and they want to do it now. Consequently, instead of receiving God's blessing, they only get what they can achieve. Waiting always involves a choice, and I would rather wait an eternity for God's solution to my problem than seek to solve it on my own. There is no comparison to the joy that comes from waiting versus rushing ahead of the Lord.

Realize God is doing a new work in your life. He does not always work the same way. He never changes, and His principles remain the same; however, He is very creative and may work one way today but another tomorrow. Therefore, ask Him to make you sensitive to His Spirit's leading. You can also pray that He will close before you every door that is not the one He wants you to pass through. When you have an open and willing heart, He will provide the wisdom you need to do His will.

Recognize that God has a plan for the storm you are facing. As we have said several times, He has a purpose for every problem you face. But you must be willing to discover this, and many times He won't reveal it immediately.

Recall His promises to you in the past. God often gives a promise to us, but we forget about it. He promised David that one day he would be king of Israel. David never forgot this, although he had to wait years to see it fulfilled. The time he spent waiting was used to prepare him to reign. You have no idea what God is preparing you to do. All you can see are your immediate circumstances. In times of prayer, you may have sensed God saying, "I have something that I want You to do. It will be a tremendous blessing." He may even reveal some of His plan to you. However, the days of waiting and wondering drag on. They become weeks, and the weeks become months. Still, there is no change in your situation. You have a promise, but you wonder if you really heard from God or from yourself. You can ask God to reaffirm His will. The psalmist writes, "The steps of a man are established by the LORD, and He delights in his way. When he falls, he will not be hurled headlong, because the LORD is the One who holds his hand" (Ps. 37:23–24).

Living the Christian life in our own strength is a waste of time. God brought the apostle Paul to a point where he cried out, "Wretched man that I am! Who will set me free from the body of this death? Thanks be to God through Jesus Christ our Lord!" (Rom. 7:24–25). Christ is the only one who can strip away the dross in our lives that is preventing us from being what God wants us to be. As I have said earlier, the process of brokenness is painful, and the depth of the pain depends on what God is seeking to remove from your life. Never overlook the fact that He has an objective that He wants you to reach. When you do, you also will reach your full potential. The problem you are facing may seem so great that you feel you will perish under its weight, but you won't. He is in the process of shattering your old self-made life so that you may walk with Him in oneness.

He also allows us to face difficulty in order to prepare us for greater service. Wheat cannot be used until it has been sifted—winnowed by the wind and separated. We cannot expect to go through life without facing times of trouble and difficulty. And the adversity that does come our way may not be a result of anything we have done wrong. After his conversion, many of the problems Paul faced came as a direct result of his devotion to Christ and also because he lived in a broken world like us. Therefore, the entire Christian life is woven tightly together with the process of brokenness. He stretches us and breaks apart our selfishness—not to harm us, but so that He can bless us.

Each one of us has watched believers go through deep valley times and wondered, *How can they do this?* The answer is, they are not doing it. God is living through them. He is bearing the weight of their burden because they have come to a point where they have stopped struggling with the difficulty and are allowing Him to carry them through the storm. Jesus told His disciples, "Let's go over to the other side of the lake" (Mark 4:35). David wrote, "Even though I walk through the valley of the shadow of death" (Ps. 23:4). In times of extreme stress and difficulty, it may seem as though you will not reach the other side or that the valley walls will come crashing in on you, but God's sovereign, omnipotent hand is always shelter-ing you—protecting and guiding you.

There are several aspects to brokenness that many people overlook.

God only breaks us in love. The entire process of broken-ness is an expression of God's love for you. Many people ask, "Lord, why would You allow this to happen to me?" Remember how we asked this same question in the opening of this chap-ter about the apostle Paul? How could God allow Paul to suf-fer such severe trials, especially when he was so committed to Christ? There is nothing within the process of brokenness that speaks of punishment. The day that Paul accepted Christ as his Savior on the Damascus Road, his sins were forgiven. His suffering was not a result of sin. God breaks us so that we will change and open our hearts up to the fullness of His love. He allows the thorns of life to prick our lives, not for the pur-pose of harming us, but instead to teach us the need for total dependence on Him.

God always sets a limitation to our brokenness. I mentioned this earlier. When God begins to target an area in our lives, He does not turn us over to the enemy and withdraw His hand of protection. The fact is, He does the opposite. He sets limita-tions on the brokenness that we experience. This includes the length of time along with the intensity of pain we feel. He never abandons us to the process but watches over us and pro-tects us. Even though we may feel at times as if we will perish, God holds our lives in His hands. He targets the area that needs attention. He arranges the circumstances. He chooses the tools, and He controls the process.

God's process of brokenness stops at the point when your will becomes broken. He will never break your spirit—only your resistant will. This is the area of your life where rebellion seeks shelter from God's omniscience. It is an area where sin lurks, waiting for a safe opportunity to resurface. King Saul is a perfect example of this. He could have reigned over Israel for many more years, but he lost the throne to David because deep within his life was a thread of rebellion. And this prevented him from reaching his full potential and carrying on the work that God had called him to do. Even though Saul fought to conceal his pride and self-gratification, God knew his heart. It was never fully turned toward Him. David's, however, was.

My personal advice to those who are going through a serious time of growth or conviction is to surrender to God. Over the course of a lifetime, each one of us will experience times of brokenness—brokenness as a form of godly discipline and brokenness as a result of something that needs to be eradicated from our lives. God made David wait many years before he became king. However, his young heart never grew resentful or prideful. He remained steadfastly committed to receiving God's promise at the right time. Do you have this type of commitment—a commitment that is steadfast and not altered by the circumstances surrounding you? Acquiring this is all a matter of developing a heart-focus for

God. Stay focused on God and not what you think "should" happen, and you will be able to wait for God's provision with a great sense of peace and victory.

The process of brokenness ceases at the point where, if it continued, it would damage God's greater purpose for your life. The Lord limits our time spent in brokenness. Nothing pleases God's heart more than a heart that is humbled before Him. So many people resist God. They don't understand that obedience is a doorway to blessing. Those who love Him will obey Him. The blessings that come from brokenness are not necessarily material, but they are eternal and far more valuable than anything else you can own. You cannot purchase the type of peace that comes from obeying God on a store shelf. Likewise, you cannot buy the infinite joy that comes from hearing God say, "Well done, My faithful servant." You can rush after the trappings of this world and lose all you receive, or you can worship God, live for Him, and gain eternity.

God uses brokenness to deepen our understanding of Him. Believe it or not, you may come to a point in seasons of brokenness when you will not want it to end. This happens not because you enjoy experiencing heartache and trial but because if you allow God to work completely in your life, you will draw closer to Him than you imagined possible. He takes us through the breaking process and strips away the very things upon which we depend. Then we gain a new perspective of Him and His love and about what He wants to do in our lives. He removes the clamor and clutter so we can hear His voice. He tells us, "For as the heavens are higher than the earth, so are My ways higher than your ways and My thoughts than your thoughts" (Isa. 55:9).

Once we allow brokenness the space to work, clarity comes. The reality of His forgiveness helps us to understand that His love is not based on anything we have done or will do in the future. It is an unconditional gift He gives to those who profess their faith in Him. God's goal is straight-forward: His brokenness is bringing us into an intimate oneness with Him. The principle of brokenness will lift almighty God, the cross, God's grace, and the shed blood of the Lord Jesus Christ to a higher level in your life. Not only will your view of God change, your view of others will also. Thoughts of selfishness will begin to fade. Tenderness will increase. Your critical, negative spirit will soften, and you will begin to want to help others with no thought of pay-back because you realize that God will never require a pay-back from you.

God never deserts us in seasons of brokenness. This point is very important because there will be times when the emo-tional or physical pain becomes so great that you will want to cry out asking God why He has abandoned you. Suffering can be intense and overwhelming. There have been times in my life when I thought, *God, have You deserted me?* I know better, but this is what I felt at the moment, and more than likely, someone reading these words is at that very point. God is right where you are.

When brokenness finally comes, God may separate you from everything you hold as valuable and dear. It is just you and God. But He is more than enough. He is sufficient to meet all your needs. He also wants you to keep in mind that maintaining healthy relationships with others is essential. Healthy relationships are ones in which everyone involved is completely committed and devoted to Jesus Christ. We learn to lean on God first but value the love and concern of friends. When we are in right relationships, we do not pressure others to meet our demands. Instead, we know deep inside that God is at work, and He will answer our prayers.

God is always patient with us in times of brokenness. God knows exactly what you are experiencing, whether you are dealing with a problem that has come as a result of sin or something that is a part of your life through no fault of your own. He knows, He sees, and He is patient with you even when you feel overwhelmed, angry, and isolated. He sees an end to your suffering. He knows the blessing that is on the way. Jesus was totally misunderstood, along with most of the disciples following His death. The apostle Paul was stoned and left for dead outside the city of Lystra. However, he did not think of himself personally but viewed God's calling on his life more important than what men thought of him. "Jews came from Antioch and Iconium, and having won over the crowds, they stoned Paul and dragged him out of the city, supposing him to be dead. But while the disciples stood around him, he got up and entered the city. The next day he went away with Barnabas to Derbe" (Acts 14:19–20).

This experience, among others, had to be very humiliating for a man of such strong character and personality. However, the level of Paul's faith was not affected. He got up and went back into the city. More important, he did not allow this incident to stop him from doing God's will. Many times, Satan will seek to trip us up by motivating someone we may know well to question our character. When this happens, we must think quickly and wisely, and focus only on Jesus. The greater your potential is for usefulness, the more you may suffer. Problems and trials come because God has something He wants you to do—something that no one else can do. It is dangerous to rebel against God. In fact, if you continue to fight and push against Him, ultimately He will set you aside—literally on a shelf where you do not have an opportunity to serve Him or enjoy the many pleasures of this life.

Years ago, I knew a middle-aged man who decided that he did not need to attend church any longer. Each Sunday, his wife and children would head out the door, but he remained behind. He thought, *I'll get back into the habit of going again at some point, but I work hard and just need to rest on the weekends.* Time passed, and he began to notice that he was not doing well physically. He felt unusually tired and could not sleep. His doctor prescribed sleeping medication, and when that did not help, he wrote the man a prescription for depression. If there was a death in the family, the man was the first one to say, "We need to go to church together." But then his desire would weaken, and after one or two Sundays, he would fall back into his old habit. He never really became serious about God even though God was very serious about him. So many of the health issues people face today come as a result of guilt, shame, and anxiety over the future. The Lord says, "Come to Me, all who are weary and heavy-laden, and I will give you rest. . . . For My yoke is easy and My burden is light."

God will lead you to victory through brokenness. Young or old, God has a purpose for your life. The first step to reach His goal is to open your life up to Him. Ask Him if there is anything within you that needs His attention. He may bring something to mind, or He may not. When brokenness does come, always remember that for the believer, it is an expression of God's love and never a form of punishment. It always leads to victory because it always leads to a closer relationship with the Lord Jesus Christ.

CHAPTER 12

You Have Always Been Loved

I can imagine dusty cracks of light filtered down into the pit where Daniel was held captive. There probably was just enough light for him to look through the darkness of his cell into the eyes of hungry lions pacing back and forth, watching their potential prey. As the darkness of night fell around him, all light was gone, and he could no longer see what surrounded him. But he could still hear the footfalls of his would-be attackers. We can imagine his heart beating hard against the inside of his chest as he weighed his options. There were not many. He could not run. There was no way of escape. Shouting would not work—it would only draw more attention, and he refused to listen to the negative thoughts that were seeking to break into his mind.

Had he not been obedient? Did he not love God? Was it not obvious that faith to him was more than idle chatter? Yes. Therefore, he was determined to wait for God's deliverance. In fact, he would wait forever if necessary for God's promise to unfold. Perhaps Daniel stood with arms lifted toward heaven in worship to God, or maybe he knelt in prayer. We are not given these details, but what we do know is that Daniel's faith and love for God was not shaken by the nature of his circumstances.

When Our Faith Is Tested

Have you ever been in a difficult situation and felt tempted to disobey God because life had become too hard for you to endure? At some point, we all have had our backs against the wall of disappointment or heartache. Most of us know what it feels like to be betrayed, rejected, or forgotten. We have heard the whispering voice of the enemy telling us that we have been treated badly, and there is no reason for us to maintain a steady sense of faith. After all, God would understand if we protested what was. *Adversity always reveals the true nature of our character.* Daniel was steady in his faith. Though he had been wrongly accused, he did not dwell on this. Instead, he set the focus of his heart on the Lord. Not once do we read that he frantically cried out to God. Certainly, he had the motivation to do this, but that did not fit the nature and character of Daniel's life. He knew that God was aware of his circumstances, and while he did not know what would happen next, he was willing to trust God for the outcome because he had an unshakable promise buried deep within his heart. He believed that God would protect him even in times of grave trouble. But should he die, Daniel knew that he would stand in God's presence and see His glory.

Daniel had an eternal perspective. His focus had never been

on the wishes or desires of men. He obeyed those in authority over him. However, he refused to worship anyone other than the Lord. God honored his faithfulness by preserving his life. Notice that God did not prevent His prophet from spending a night in the lions' den. He allowed Daniel to be tested, and He allows the same thing to happen in our lives to bring us to the same point that he reached: God is ever faithful, and when we trust Him, He will solve every problem we face.

He could have become paralyzed with fear. Not only was his life on the line, but his future was too. Darius had signed a decree. The only person or thing that was to be worshiped was the king himself. Daniel, however, did what he normally did—he worshiped the Lord and no one else. His faith was tried in the crucible of adversity. God used this situation to purify Daniel's faith, and there will be times when He does the same thing in our lives. He stretches us and allows us to face difficulty—not to terrify us—but to strengthen us and purify us so we will become a reflection of His hope to others.

No Need to Fear

There was no reason for Daniel to be afraid. He had obeyed God perfectly. When we obey God, we do not have to worry about what will happen tomorrow. God has taken care of all of our tomorrows. However, if we are living outside of His will in sin, then we can expect to face some really difficult times. While He loves us with an everlasting love, God hates sin, and He wants us to hate it too. In Psalm 97:10, He commands us to "hate evil, you who love the LORD." And in Psalm 37:27, He admonishes us to "depart from evil and do good, so you will abide forever."

Sin causes a separation in our fellowship with God, and this sense of separation gives birth to fear. Deep within our spirits, we know what we have done is wrong. Guilt builds, and we want to hide from God rather than enjoy being in His presence. This is exactly what happened in the garden of Eden when Adam and Eve sinned against God. They became fearful and hid from His presence (Gen. 3:7–10). Even when we sin, God does not stop loving us. He created us out of His love. His greatest desire is to have fellowship with us. Sin is the one thing that prevents this from happening. When we yield to temptation and step away from what we know is right, we suffer the consequences of our decision. Yet, when we pray and seek His forgiveness, He offers it to us just as He gives His unconditional grace and mercy freely.

Few people have had to endure a night alone in a lions' den where the stench of death is so strong that it is difficult to breathe. Plus, the lions used for this type of punishment usually were starved in advance so that they would hit their prey fast and tear it apart. However, Daniel escaped untouched. His life was spared and has become a testimony of faith—one that even King Darius was quick to acknowledge.

When problems escalate, you can do one of two things.

You can ask God to give you the ability to remain steadfast in your faith, trusting Him to provide exactly what you need when you need it. Or you can become doubtful, fearful, and worried. Always remember, God is fully aware of your circumstances, and His commitment to you never changes. What He has promised, He will do. In her devotional classic *Streams in the Desert,* Mrs. Charles Cowman reminds us, "Sometimes, God sends severe blasts of trial upon His children to develop their graces. Just as torches burn most brightly when swung to and fro; just as the juniper plant smells sweetest when flung into the flames; so the richest qualities of a Christian often come out under the north wind of suffering and adversity. Bruised hearts often emit the fragrance that God loveth to smell."

Adversity provides the perfect opportunity for us to allow Him to stretch our faith, take us to new places of blessing, and prepare us for victories beyond anything we can imagine. Elijah, like Daniel, was severely tested. He had no idea that God was preparing him for a tremendous conquest—Mount Carmel loomed in his not-so-distant future (1 Kings 18). This was the very place where God demonstrated His greatest power to those who worshiped Baal. Many times, when we are in the middle of God's will and following His plan, He will require us to face a season of testing. A deeper level of faith and devotion usually requires time spent in darkness with Him. What is He requiring of you during this time of trial? Has He asked you to go to a place that seems far from your home? Do not worry. Do not be frightened. He is with you, and He will not leave you alone.

When the Brook Runs Dry

At first, there was plenty of water in the brook where God had led Elijah to set up camp (1 Kings 17:2–5). The Lord commanded the birds of the air to feed His prophet. Many scholars tell how Elijah was fed by ravens—animals that were scavengers. Regardless of the method, God provided for His prophet. Elijah lacked nothing; then one day the brook began to dry up, and the Lord instructed him to leave that place. Most people find it extremely difficult to stay put when everything around them is falling apart, or in Elijah's case, the brook is running dry. They grow restless and want to do something to escape the trouble. Even when many people are forced to stay in one place, such as a job they find stressful, they may run away emotionally. But notice how the prophet waited until God made it clear that it was time to move. He lived by a dwindling brook for many days until he heard the Lord's voice instructing him to move on to another location. When it came, he packed up his bedroll and left the brook of Cherith.

The Lord had a greater purpose in mind for Elijah's suffering. He was preparing His prophet for the day he would stand on Mount Carmel and face the prophets of Baal (1 Kings 18:20–40). He also was training Elijah to see

Him as the source of every need he had. In times of difficulty, people may reach out to help us. While we are deeply grateful, we also should be keenly aware that only Christ is our Provider. Just as ravens fed Elijah, God may use others to meet our needs. However, these birds were not Elijah's providers. The brook certainly was not. There was only one Person who could meet his needs, and that was God.

People get into trouble when they look to others to solve their problems. God is our problem solver. He allowed the difficulty, but He will also provide the answer that you need for the right solution. The answer will not come from your supervisor, friends, family members, or even through a paycheck. Our provision comes only from God. Someone reading this book may have lost everything within the past few months. You may be discouraged, but you have a future that is brimming with hope; however, it does not rest in the arrival of a check or the rebuilding of a home or a family. It rests in your ability to trust God in the hard times just as much as you trust Him in times of joy and celebration.

Far too often, people depend on worldly "brooks" and "ravens" to meet their needs. This was Israel's main problem. They did not look to God as their provider. When trouble came, they cried out to Him; but after He had solved their problem, they returned to trusting in their own abilities. If we become comfortable in circumstances that are outside of God's will, then they can become our security and not God. Even believers living for the Lord can do the same thing.

They may become frightened over the thought of having to change jobs. They would rather stay where they are than risk a change. God has a way of drying up our brooks to move us on to greater blessings. What looks like an ending to us is really a new beginning to Him.

We may mistakenly think that if the water dries up, then we will die; but this is never the case with God. His resources are inexhaustible. His love for us is eternal, and His future plan for us is mighty and full of hope and promise. Therefore, never give up. Though you may be facing the darkest time of your life, if you will ask Him to cover you with a sense of His closeness, you will sense streams of light flowing down into your circumstances. You never know just how close you are to being released from the agony you are feeling.

When You Are Tempted to Give Up—Don't!

Peter had been arrested and thrown into jail. By this point in his life, he knew what happened to men and women who worshiped Christ. However, he had learned many lessons of faith and believed that no matter what came next, Jesus was with him, and he would not cave in to fear or disbelief.

> On the very night when Herod was about to bring him forward, Peter was sleeping between two soldiers, bound with two chains, and guards in front of the door were watching

over the prison. . . . Behold, an angel of the Lord suddenly appeared and a light shone in the cell; and he struck Peter's side and woke him up, saying, "Get up quickly." And his chains fell off his hands.

And the angel said to him, "Gird yourself and put on your sandals." And he did so. And he said to him, "Wrap your cloak around you and follow me." And he went out and continued to follow, and he did not know that what was being done by the angel was real, but thought he was seeing a vision. When they had passed the first and second guard, they came to the iron gate that leads into the city, which opened for them by itself; and they went out and went along one street, and immediately the angel departed from him. When Peter came to himself, he said, "Now I know for sure that the Lord has sent forth His angel and rescued me." (Acts 12:6–11)

God wants to rescue you, to give you hope and a sense of a bright future. No matter how small or large, when difficulty comes, call out to Him because He is the One who is committed to solving every problem and supplying every need you have. Tell Him your need and your situation, and ask Him to provide the wisdom and encouragement you need to get through this trouble. When you commit your way to Him, the prison doors will open, and His light of hope and love will fill your heart and mind. He will show you exactly how to walk through each and every day as you place your trust in Him.

ABOUT THE AUTHOR

Through his 50 years of ministry, Dr. Charles F. Stanley has become known as "America's Pastor" for his dedication to leading people worldwide into a growing relationship with Jesus Christ. Dr. Stanley is the founder and president of In Touch Ministries, whose *In Touch* radio and television program can be heard around the world in more than 100 languages. He has also been Senior Pastor of First Baptist Church in Atlanta, Georgia since 1971.

Dr. Stanley received his bachelor of arts degree from the University of Richmond, his bachelor of divinity degree from Southwestern Baptist Theological Seminary, and his master's degree and doctorate from Luther Rice Seminary. He has twice been elected president of the Southern Baptist Convention and is a *New York Times* best-selling author, having written more than 50 books, including *Living the Extraordinary Life, When the Enemy Strikes, Finding Peace, God Is In Control, Pathways to His Presence, Success God's Way, Charles Stanley's Handbook for Christian Living, The Source of My Strength, How to Listen to God, Life Principles Bible,* and his latest release, *Landmines in the Path of the Believer.*

Informative.

Insightful.

Inspiring.

Invigorating.

In Touch Magazine.

If you like Dr. Stanley's books, television broadcast and radio program, you'll love his award-winning publication. *In Touch* magazine is full of informative resources that will strengthen your faith, including: daily devotionals from Dr. Stanley's sermons, in-depth Bible studies, inspirational articles by well-known Christian authors, and insightful feature stories that will encourage your family and support your relationship with Jesus Christ.

Best of all, it's *free*. Have *In Touch* magazine delivered to your home or office every month as a gift from Dr. Stanley and In Touch Ministries. *In Touch* magazine has been inspiring and encouraging people for more than 25 years. Subscribe today and experience a publication that enriches the spiritual lives of one million readers every month. Call 1-800-IN-TOUCH, or visit InTouch.org

Do you ever wish you could have more of In Touch at your fingertips?

Dr. Stanley and In Touch Ministries are just a click away. Find exactly what you need faster and easier than ever before at *InTouch.org*.

Log on now to:

- Watch and listen to Dr. Stanley's messages.
- Read daily devotions and inspiring articles from *In Touch* magazine.
- Get answers to your questions about God.
- Download In Touch Podcasts.
- Support In Touch by donating online.
- Discover how to have a life full of joy and purpose.
- Shop at the easy-to-use online bookstore.
- Find strength to help you through difficult times.
- See how In Touch is reaching people around the world.
- Learn how you can make a difference in your own home and community.
- Enjoy special online offers.

In Touch's mission is to lead people worldwide into a growing relationship with Jesus Christ and to strengthen the local church. Whether you're a new believer or a mature Christian, InTouch.org can help you draw closer to God. Log on to *InTouch.org* today and take advantage of all the great things In Touch Ministries has to offer.